HEALING

BETRAYAL TRAUMA

The Biblical Secret to Restoring Your Heart, Rebuilding Trust, and Finding the Peace You Deserve

MIKE VESTIL

TABLE OF CONTENTS

A NOTE FOR YOU, THE READER

Thank you for choosing this book. Healing after betrayal takes courage, and I know how much confusion and pain can surface when you begin the process of rebuilding trust. That's why I created a few simple tools to walk with you as you heal.

As a gift for reading, you can download a free companion toolkit here: **mikevestil.com/healingbetrayal-gift (or scan the QR code below)**

SCAN ME

Inside, you'll find:

1. Rebuilding Trust Checklist — practical and spiritual steps to begin trusting again.
2. Betrayal Detox Journal — guided journal prompts to release anger, shame, and self-blame.
3. The 5 Stages of Heart Restoration Journal — scripture-based reflections to guide you from shock to surrender.
4. 7 Healing Prayers for the Betrayed Heart — short, honest prayers for the days you can't find words.

These are the same tools I wish I had when I was learning how to trust again. I hope they help you take small, steady steps toward peace, freedom, and a renewed faith in the goodness of love.

With all my love and hope for you,

Mike Vestil

INTRODUCTION:

THE TEEPEE IN SPAIN

The first night in Málaga, Spain, I sat cross-legged on a woven rug inside a teepee pitched on a terraced hillside. Out here, the mountains fell away into miles of olive trees, and the silver undersides of their leaves flashed in the wind like fish. The air smelled like sage and cedar.

Someone had strung small glass lanterns along the central pole of the teepee, and the light quivered each time the canvas breathed. Twenty of us formed a circle around that glimmering central pole.

Behind the canvas, a goat's bell clinked somewhere down the slope. Someone's kettle hissed. The sky outside was the blue-black between sunset and night, and the Mediterranean wind came up the ravine as if to listen.

I hadn't come here expecting to heal. I thought I was here to teach, after a facilitator named Trinity had invited me. Trinity and I had met months earlier in Bali. She had wandered into a tiny mastermind I was leading for creative entrepreneurs. Imagine ten people at a long wooden table, barefoot and sweating in the humid air, while a storm shook the palm leaves like a dog with a toy. She liked that I could talk about business and finance in one breath and then pivot to soul and spirituality in the next. "Come share your wisdom," she said later. "I'm hosting a retreat in Spain. We'll cover healing and relationships in the mornings, and I'd love to have you run a business lab in the afternoons."

I said *yes* before I knew why. *Yes,* because it felt like movement. *Yes,* because the ocean between me and my old life still wasn't big enough, and Spain was another horizon I could put between myself and heartache. I bought the ticket like a curtain is drawn, thinking it would be the end of one part of my story.

To be honest, I didn't land in Bali for business. I fled there. A few years before I arrived at this teepee, my girlfriend back in the United States sat across from me in our favorite restaurant and told me she had cheated on me. No matter how much time seemed to pass, I still couldn't get the feeling of betrayal out of my body. I still remember the moment when she told me. Her voice was flat. No tears. No tremor. She said it the way some people say, "It looks like rain."

I remember the sound the fans in the room made. I remember the click of the air conditioning turning on and how suddenly it felt too cold in the room. I remember that my hands rested open on my knees, and that I had a strange awareness of how far my hands were from the rest of me, as if they belonged to a person I could not quite reach.

When she finished speaking, I felt something inside me drop through a trapdoor. Not rage. Not even grief at first. Just the sensation that the structure holding my life in place had suddenly disappeared like a tablecloth jerked out from under a set of dishes. The plates didn't move. The table remained where it was. But everything was rattling, and I could not stop the sound. The betrayal hurt so bad. My heart was destroyed. Not only did I lose trust in her, the person I had trusted for the past 4 years of my life. I also lost my trust in myself.

How could I be so blind? I mean, here I was sacrificing my health to build a life that could hold our future together. A life where we could build a family. A life where we didn't have to repeat our parents' mistakes. I trusted her with everything. When I found out about the betrayal, I felt disgusted. I didn't know what to think. Part of me wanted to think this was just a cruel joke or a bad dream. It was not. The emotions were too much for me to handle. So, I did what I thought would be best. I left. I left not just the relationship, but the country.

I left for Thailand first, because it was easy to get there from Chicago. Then I left Thailand for Bali, because people said the island knows how to hold a broken heart without asking it to sing.

In Bali, I woke before dawn, drank coffee that tasted like earth and chocolate, and walked the rice terraces until my calves burned. I read passages from a small Bible I brought from home, the thin paper bruised with old underlines: *The Lord is close to the broken-hearted.* I nodded like a stubborn child who's trying to be soothed and won't admit it's working.

On the island, my life became simple: *sweat, prayer, page.* I wrote down dreams and memories as if I could stitch them together into something that explained me to me. I met with a life coach who asked gentle questions and then let silence do the heavy lifting. It was in one of those silences that something old began to speak. Not her betrayal, but the echo that made it feel familiar.

The way the ground had disappeared beneath me felt like a part of my childhood. I could trace the line: the tense peace at dinner with my parents; the unspoken words; the way love in my house meant understanding things correctly and not needing too much. I had learned to read a room like scripture and to treat my own needs like temptations.

I realized it wasn't bad luck that led me to keep loving people who couldn't love me back without hurting me. It was muscle memory. I didn't fall in love with what was healthy. I fell in love with what felt familiar.

When Trinity invited me to Spain, I agreed because I felt a strong urge to continue moving forward. I packed a small journal, a few changes of clothes, a gray hoodie, and my well-worn Bible. I boarded a flight with a carry-on and a promise to myself that I would go as a helper. If I kept my hands busy serving others, maybe I could ignore the parts of me that were still bleeding.

Then, I was sitting on the ground inside a teepee with twenty strangers breathing in the same room as if we'd been born to form a circle. Trinity opened with a bell and a whisper. She had that calm voice facilitators use when the room is stiff with stories that haven't yet learned how to be told.

"We'll go one by one," Trinity said. "Say your name, where you're from, and what you hope to leave here with."

The woman to my left went first. "I'm from Manchester," she said, picking at the edge of her shawl. "I want to stop apologizing for breathing."

A man from Berlin wanted to stop waking at 3 a.m. with his jaw locked.

A nurse from Toronto wanted to trust herself around people who said they loved her.

Then it was my turn. "I'm Mike," I said. "I'm here to help with the business labs." It sounded thin as it left my mouth. I added, "But I think I'm also here to learn how to be a person again." A few people smiled, the way you do when you hear a truth that isn't polished.

Around the circle, three faces held my attention the way anchors hold boats.

The first was a woman named Sarah. She was mid-thirties, with a softness that had survived a hard season. She kept tucking her hair behind her ear as though it helped her gather her courage.

"I'm from Dallas," she said. "Mother of two." Her voice steadied. "I left a marriage that the church said I should hold together. But the marriage was holding me like a knife. It held me because he betrayed me with another woman, and I didn't know what to do."

"At first, I tried to please him more. That only destroyed the boundaries more, boundaries I did not know how to handle. When I lost trust in my husband, I lost trust in God as well. I don't know how that could happen, but it did. My love for God and my love for my husband both became invisible... and so did I."

She exhaled like a diver surfacing. "I want to learn how to trust myself and God again, without feeling like I'm betraying Him."

Emily was in her late twenties, with bright eyes that seemed to ask questions. "Atlanta," she said, a quick smile that didn't hide the tremor in her fingers. "I'm the cycle-breaker in my family. That's what my therapist says, anyway. I don't want my kids to inherit our silence someday."

7

"I am here," she said, almost breathless, "not because of a partner. I don't have one. What I do have is an alcoholic father. He controlled every second of the day in our house. I tried to control the results of that, to keep the peace, but it was like trying to shovel a blizzard off of a sidewalk with a teaspoon. Completely ineffective, though I never stopped trying."

"The pain never really leaves me. It's not only an emotional experience; it's a physical one. I want to understand how I can feel this way. How does that make sense?" Her eyes shone. "I want to be free enough to teach my future children what freedom is." She started to tear up. These were not performative tears, they were the kind that hover but don't fall because you're busy holding everything else.

Mary was in her fifties, her hands strong from years of caregiving. "Kentucky," she said. "I came because my counselor told me this would be good for me. I keep feeling guilty for wanting peace."

"My husband ruled the house. He liked me for what I could do for him, but I eventually realized he had no interest in me as an actual person. If I asked for anything, he resisted. He would answer me with scripture when I longed for simple kindness. The rest of the time, he simply ignored me."

"No matter how much I tried to obey him, he still took no notice. And though I love God, when I found out about the other woman he was seeing, it broke the ground that I was standing on. I mean, what a hypocrite. How can a person not care for my feelings that much? I just don't know how to handle it. Our family and our kids looked so perfect from the outside, but inside, the pressure was destroying me. I began to withdraw from everything... from home, from church, from the world in general. It was as though everything within me simply closed up shop. Worse, no one even noticed."

If you've ever been in a room where people decide to tell the truth, you know that the air changes. It gets heavier and kinder at the same time. The teepee canvas moved with the wind. Someone's bracelet chimed each time she shifted her weight. Beyond the hill, the last orange seam of daylight went dark.

We closed the first circle with candles. "We'll begin in the morning," Trinity said. "Rest. Drink water. Let this place start to work on you."

✦ ✦ ✦

That first night, I couldn't sleep. The mind does a strange thing when it's safe enough to remember: It starts offering you reels you didn't ask to see.

I watched the moment of betrayal in my head again, but this time, the sound was off like an old movie.

I saw my mother cutting fruit at the counter when I was seven, and the way her smile shut like a door because my dad walked into the room asking for another can of beer.

I saw myself at twelve, laughing too loudly to prove I wasn't in the way.

I saw my face the day I boarded the flight to Bangkok, trying to look brave for nobody in particular.

I prayed a small prayer that I had prayed a hundred times in Bali: "God, I don't know where to put this." The answer was not a sentence but a sensation, the kind you feel behind your ribs: *For now, put it here.*

I fell asleep with my hand flat over my chest, as if holding a page in a book I meant to return to.

✦ ✦ ✦

Morning broke bright. The mountains wore that early light that makes you forgive the night for existing.

We met on the terrace. A line of mugs steamed along a wooden table, and someone had cut oranges that tasted like the color they were. Birds stitched the air with thread-thin calls.

We began with breath. Inhale for four seconds, hold for four seconds, exhale for six seconds. The body, like a good horse, calms when given cues. Trinity read a short passage about grief, pain, and sorrow, and how naming pain is not the opposite of faith but its expression.

Then the sharing deepened. The circle became a living archive of betrayal in its many dialects.

One woman's fiancé had called off the wedding by text message.

A man raised in a house of shouting had learned to mistake adrenaline for love and wondered why kind women felt "boring" to him.

A pastor's daughter said she couldn't tell whether she feared God or feared disappointing everyone who claimed to speak for Him.

When it was my turn, I surprised myself. I didn't share a thesis. I shared the small sound my heart made when I heard words I couldn't unknow. How I felt when I found out she betrayed me. I said how it wasn't just her voice I heard in that moment; it was a chorus. The chorus of a boy who learned that being easy to love is safer than being honest. The chorus of a man who picked partners like mirrors for his worth. I expressed my concerns about whether I could truly heal my heart, rebuild trust in both myself and others, and achieve the peace in my relationship that I desperately desired before starting a family.

I said I was tired of being loved for the version of me who never needed anything. My hands shook. I tucked them under my thighs like a kid.

It's strange how quickly strangers stop being strangers when a room commits to truth. By lunch, I knew which laugh belonged to which person across the terrace. I knew who would cut their sandwich in half to share. I knew who would line up mats a few extra inches apart because closeness felt expensive.

✦ ✦ ✦

That afternoon, I was supposed to lead the business lab. Trinity put a hand on my shoulder before the session. "Teach if you'd like," she said. "Or don't." It wasn't permission to abandon my role. It was permission to notice I was in one.

I taught briefly about building businesses and leadership. We discussed offers and boundaries, about choosing your *yes* so your *no* stays holy.

However, I kept catching Sarah's eyes and the way she looked down when I said the word *boundary*. I kept thinking of Emily scribbling notes like the words might evaporate if she didn't grab them. I kept seeing Mary straighten her spine as if she wanted to be tall, but her past kept asking her to fold.

✦ ✦ ✦

That night, we returned to the teepee. Someone put a drum on the floor beside the lanterns.

We wrote letters we didn't intend to send. We read a psalm out loud together, the kind that starts in the valley and crawls toward the hill: *He heals the broken-hearted and binds up their wounds.*

No one tried to fix anyone. We let the words do their work the way balm works: slow, persistent, and unflashy.

✦ ✦ ✦

Over the next few days, the retreat found its rhythm. Mornings were for story, scripture, and breath. Afternoons were dedicated to learning and walking through the orchard. Evenings provided a kind of silence that doesn't ask questions but answers them simply by being present.

I realized I was not there to hide inside my competence. I was there to be disarmed by kindness.

I watched Sarah one morning as she told the group how she'd learned to evaluate herself through the mood of a man. "If he was quiet," she said, "I became a weather app. I'd rerun the week and try to locate the storm inside me that caused his forecast." She started to cry, quickly, like someone who's embarrassed to show tears in public. "I'm so tired of checking the temperature before I decide who I'm allowed to be."

We didn't offer solutions. We let the sentence sit like a prayer that had finally found a mouth.

Emily said she was worried she'd bring her family's silence into her future. "I want to be a mother one day," she said, "but I'm scared I'll teach a child to swallow what should be said out loud." She looked at me. "How do you unlearn a thing that taught you how to survive?"

I shared with her what someone told me in Bali. "You practice telling the truth in safe places, on ordinary days, so your body learns the difference between danger and honesty."

She wrote it down as if I'd handed her a key.

Mary told us how church felt like a house where everyone took off their shoes and lined them up neatly, while she tracked in mud and apologized for the dirt of being human. "I love Jesus!" she said, with a ferocity that made me sit up straighter. "I just don't know how to love myself without feeling like I'm breaking a rule."

We looked at the lanterns for a long time after she said it. Sometimes, God answers by letting your confession hang above a room like a banner.

✦ ✦ ✦

By the third day, I understood what this book needed to be. Not a lecture. Not a list. A circle you could put in your hands. A teepee of pages.

As we walked through Spain, we faced deep issues of betrayal and emotional abuse. We saw the selfish patterns that often show up in relationships and reflected on the burdens we carry from the past.

We also found the strength to break free from them. The difficult math of forgiveness was on our minds, along with the importance of setting boundaries. We noticed how shame can fade away, while the need for control can feel heavy and confining. In the end, we welcomed the slow journey of finding redemption that awaits us.

Each chapter would open like a door to one of those nights in the teepee, where someone would light a candle and a story would begin. Each chapter would pair lived experiences with scripture, not as a weapon but as water. Not to argue you into healing, but to sit with you until hope could stand on its own legs.

✦ ✦ ✦

On the last night of the retreat, the wind came hard. The teepee strained and then settled, like a chest exhaling.

We passed around slips of paper with things we were ready to release, written in small, careful letters. Some burned theirs in a steel bowl. Some folded theirs into their Bibles. I buried mine under a flat stone by the rosemary bush. I prayed a simple prayer over the dirt. "God, grow something here that looks like peace."

Before we left, Sarah hugged me. It was a hug with weight, the kind where you can feel a person decide to trust you. "I don't feel crazy anymore," she said. "I just feel... new."

Emily slipped a note into my journal that said, "When I have a daughter one day, I want to read her parts of this week."

Mary squeezed my hand and met my eyes in the way that only women who have shouldered decades of abuse do. "I think God is gentler than I was told," she said. "I think that's the truth I'm taking home."

I walked down the gravel path from the teepee to my room, a lantern light bobbing in my hand. The olive trees on either side shivered silver in the wind. I could hear the ocean's hush, a sound as old as beginnings.

I thought about how I had boarded a flight for Thailand because I was afraid of what I'd lost back home. I had lost her anyway and found something truer. There was no guarantee people would stop hurting me. Not a formula, just a God who refuses to waste pain and a circle of humans who learned how to hold it.

✦ ✦ ✦

If you're holding this book, I assume something in you is tired. Maybe you're shaky with fresh betrayal. Maybe you're years out and still jumping at small sounds you can't name. Maybe you're the faithful mother, the cycle-breaker daughter, or the silent survivor who's finally decided to say something out loud. Maybe you're a man who learned to be the strong one until "strong" meant "numb."

However you got here, welcome. You don't have to perform in these pages. You don't have to shrink. You don't have to be certain. The teepee is wide enough for doubt and belief to sit side by side and share a cup of tea.

Here's what I can promise: I will not rush you. We will grieve together. We will draw boundaries without apology. We will explore forgiveness without enabling. We will celebrate the smallest wins because small wins teach your nervous system what safety feels like. Then, we will end where all good journeys end, not with a trophy but with a table. A place to sit down inside your life and call it home.

Each chapter that follows is one of the nights in that teepee. Each one is a lesson learned with my knees in the dust and my heart in my hands.

We'll begin with betrayal and how it shatters the nervous system. We'll name emotional abuse and the way words can cut deeper than fists. We'll recognize narcissism not to diagnose, but to discern. We'll trace generational trauma and bless the courage it takes to break chains you didn't forge. We'll wrestle with forgiveness, not as a loophole for evil but as liberation for the wounded. We'll practice boundaries as love with limits. We'll unmask shame and walk out of its quiet prison. We'll loosen control and learn the rest that comes from trust. And we'll close with redemption, because God doesn't stop at "better." He makes new.

If you can, read this the way we lived those nights: slowly. Let the prayers be short and honest. If you're skeptical, bring your skepticism; it's often just hope wearing armor. If you cry, good. Tears are water, and they help things grow. If you need to throw the book on the couch and take a walk, take the walk. Then come back. The circle will still be here.

✦ ✦ ✦

Before we begin, a blessing:

May the God who heals the brokenhearted meet you in these pages. May you find the courage to tell the truth and the gentleness to hear it. May your boundaries be gates, not walls, clear, strong, and kind. May what others meant for evil become, in God's hands, the seed of a good you can't yet imagine. And may you leave this circle not with a new mask, but with a new name: Free.

Welcome to the teepee. Let's begin.

A QUIET INVITATION

Before we begin,

I want to offer you something gentle

for the road you're about to walk.

Healing after betrayal and emotional injury isn't
meant to be done alone.

It's not only about understanding what happened.

It's about having support, guidance, and safe places to land while
you rebuild.

On my website, you'll find multiple ways to connect, reach out, and
receive support, along with simple tools, reflections, and practical
resources to help you restore trust, strengthen boundaries, and
learn how to love safely again.

If at any point you feel overwhelmed or alone, you don't have to
carry it by yourself.

You can visit:
mikevestil.com

Take a moment now if you wish,

then come back to Chapter One.

The circle will still be here.

CHAPTER 1

BETRAYAL

WHEN TRUST SHATTERS

❧

The next morning, the mountains looked rinsed and new, as if the night had washed them in silence. Light spilled down the terraces in thin gold sheets. Someone had already set out a tray of mugs and a basket of oranges. A kettle hissed. The goat bell below the olive grove made its small, reliable sound.

Trinity rang the brass bowl with a soft strike. We gathered inside the teepee, blankets draped over knees, pads beneath us, steam rising from cups. The teepee breathed in the breeze. You could feel the room check its pulse and find a steady beat.

"We're going to sit with betrayal today," Trinity said, not so much as an announcement but as a confession. No lecture voice, just a woman naming a reality we all knew.

No one moved. We all understood that word. It was in our luggage.

She guided our breathing until the nervous flutter inside my ribs felt like a bird deciding to land. "Notice your body," she said. "What wakes up when you hear the word betrayal? Don't judge it. Just notice."

My hands went cold. The place behind my sternum hummed. Around the circle, I heard the small movements people make when they're trying not to fidget: a thumb rubbing a knuckle, fabric straightening, a quiet swallow.

"Let's speak from the body first," Trinity said. "Then we'll let the mind add its words."

A woman from Manchester reached up and touched the hollow of her throat. "Tightness," she said. "Like someone put a hand there and forgot."

The man from Berlin tapped the back of his jaw. "Clenched," he said. "At night I wake and I'm biting air."

Mary placed the palm of her hand over her heart and let it rest there. "Hollow," she whispered. "Like a room where someone moved out and left the lights on."

I felt the old drop, the trapdoor feeling I'd known in the restaurant back home. "Falling," I said. "Like stepping where the ground should be and finding nothing."

Trinity nodded and let the words settle like dust that needs to be seen before it can be swept. "Thank you," she said. "Today, if we're willing, we'll bring our stories into the light and let them speak. We will allow scripture to resonate with us, not to debate its meaning, but to accompany us on our journey. Think of this as a day to be honest about your pain."

We went around the circle, not in order, not with any rule except the one the room made together: Tell the truth you can bear to tell right now.

Sarah tucked her hair behind her ear and inhaled like she was easing into cold water. "My ex-husband had a second phone," she said. "I found it in the garage, hidden behind a box of Christmas lights."

She swallowed. "You know that moment when your hand knows before your mind does? I opened it, read messages I didn't want to read, and my body started shaking like a fire alarm." Her hands moved as if the moment were still happening. "I asked him about it. He said I was being dramatic. He told me everyone texts, and it doesn't mean anything."

"For months, I became an investigator in my own home. Then, I became a ghost. I pressed myself flat against the walls of my life so I'd stop knocking into his truth."

A tear made its way down her cheek. "When he finally told me, he did it like a man admitting he forgot to take out the trash. No emotion. That was worse than the rest. When I filed for a divorce, I felt so guilty. I didn't know how to tell my kids. I didn't know how to face my friends and family. I didn't know what story I needed to tell them. Was I supposed to lie to protect my family's image? Or do I tell people the truth and suffer from their silent judgment? Either way, I felt like a complete idiot. No matter which option I had, I felt like I would lose regardless."

No one hurried to comfort her with words. The teepee had its own way of nodding.

Emily picked at a loose thread on her sweater and then left it alone. "When it comes to the word betrayal, I think about my dad. He promised he was done drinking. He promised me when I was nine, again at thirteen, and again last Thanksgiving. He wore his promise like a medal. But promises are only as strong as the person wearing them."

She took a breath that trembled and then steadied. "I learned to count breaths at the dinner table. If he put his fork down too hard, I counted how many bites I could skip to make him laugh instead." She looked around, apologizing with her eyes for taking up space. "I'm tired of the empty promises."

A soft murmur passed through the room, not words but breath, the way people breathe when they have just witnessed something true. No one tried to soothe her. We simply held the story with her and let its weight settle in the circle like a stone finally placed on the ground instead of carried alone.

Mary didn't cry. She spoke with the quiet that comes after a storm has had its way. "I married a man who loved me like an idea," she said. "When the real me showed up, he called her demanding. He used the Bible like a ruler."

She put two fingers together and tapped them against her thigh. "When I found out about the other woman and the life that he lived without my awareness, he asked me to forgive him, but he never changed his behavior, nor did he stop seeing the other woman. I just don't know what to do. We have kids together. I don't want to break the peace."

The circle widened without moving. That's what testimony does when it's true. It makes more room.

Trinity let the lantern crackle for a moment before she began. She didn't open the Bible. She just looked at us and spoke slowly.

"One night in Gethsemane, Jesus had gone there with His disciples to pray. The air was thick with olive branches, and His closest friends were nearby, though they kept drifting off to sleep. Just hours before, they had shared the Passover meal. Jesus had even washed their feet."

She drew a quiet breath.

"One of them, Judas Iscariot, had slipped away from the table earlier. The others didn't understand why. But Judas had already made a deal with the chief priests and soldiers. He had promised to hand over Jesus in return for silver coins."

The lanternlight flickered across her face as she continued. "Judas came back into the garden, leading armed men with torches and swords. They needed a sign, a way to know which man to arrest in the shadows of the trees. So, Judas gave them this signal. *The one I kiss is the man. Arrest Him.*"

Her voice softened. "Judas walked right up to Jesus. He greeted Him like a friend, like a brother, like someone who belonged. Then he kissed Him. A kiss that should have meant love, loyalty, closeness. But this time, it was betrayal. With that kiss, soldiers stepped forward, and Jesus was taken."

Trinity let the silence stretch, the story landing heavier than any commentary could.

"The wound wasn't the ropes they tied Him with," she said finally. "It wasn't even the weapons they carried. The deepest wound was the kiss itself. Betrayal dressed up as love. That's what makes betrayal cut so deeply. It doesn't come from strangers. It comes from the ones who had access to your heart."

She looked around the circle, letting her eyes meet each of ours.

"If you feel called tonight," she said gently, "what has betrayal looked like in your story? What does this moment with Judas and Jesus teach you about how fragile trust can be and how God meets us in that kind of pain?"

The man from Berlin spoke into his fist, not to hide, but to stay steady. "It taught me to sleep with my jaw in armor."

The nurse from Toronto said, "It taught me to rehearse apologies while I brushed my teeth."

A quiet woman from Cape Town answered, "It taught me to keep my favorite parts in a box and only open it when I'm alone."

"It taught me to be perfect at guessing," Sarah said. "Not good at asking."

"It taught me to be the rescuer, even when no one was drowning," Emily added.

"It taught me to obey so hard I forgot what obedience was for," Mary said, half-smiling at the sad ingenuity of it.

Trinity let us sit inside our sentences. Then she asked us to put a hand on the body part that spoke first. "If you can, befriend it," she said. "Not with logic. With breath."

We breathed. Inhale four, hold four, exhale six. I counted the exhale like a slow-release valve hissing open. My chest obeyed before my mind did. Outside, the wind ran a hand through the grove, and the leaves flashed pale like fish turning.

"This is betrayal trauma," she said at last, not as a diagnosis, but as a name card placed at the table. "When someone we depend on breaks trust, the body's alarms don't just sound during the event. They reset the whole house. The doors are double locked. The windows get nailed shut. Floodlights stay on." She glanced around. "Shame. Anxiety. Loss of self-worth. Isolation. The consequences you feel from someone else's mistake. It's unfair."

There were nods and glances at the relief of hearing your private survival tricks spoken out loud by someone who isn't shaming you for having them.

"My friends told me to move on," the Manchester woman said. "As if grief is a hallway you run down." She laughed once, a dry sound. "I'm still in the first room."

"Me, too," I said. "And sometimes, I loop back to the door to check that it's still open."

Trinity smiled the kind of smile that forgives. "There is a time to move," she said. "But first, there's a time to mourn. Our faith knows this. Grief is not a lack of belief. It's what belief does when it refuses to pretend." She didn't pull out references; she didn't need to. The Psalms were already humming under everything.

We stood up and broke for tea. Slices of orange bled on the cutting board, and someone passed around a jar of almonds. The small human tasks of pouring, offering, and chewing brought us back into our bodies in a merciful way.

✦ ✦ ✦

When we sat down again, Trinity placed a blank page and a pencil in front of each of us. "Habits help the nervous system learn a new song," she said. "Let's try three today. A grievance, a breath, and a truth."

She set a small timer. We wrote our grievances as if we were finally allowed to speak in our native language.

I didn't try to be poetic. I wrote what was true, the plain kind of truth. *I felt dropped. I didn't see it coming. I'm still angry at how calm she was. I hate that I doubt myself. I miss the man I thought I was.*

When the timer chimed, no one collected anything. The page belonged to whoever owned the pain on it.

We breathed again. Inhale four, hold four, exhale six. "If it helps," she said, "pair the breath with a simple prayer." She offered one and let it land like a feather. "Inhale: *God is my refuge.* Exhale: *I am safe in Him.*"

The room rose and fell like a single lung. The words didn't fix anything. They made a small shelter, which felt like enough.

For the third practice, Trinity asked us to write a sentence of truth under the grievances. Not toxic positivity or slogans; just a sentence that refuses to let the wound define everything.

I stared at the paper until the words showed up. *This betrayal happened to me. It is not my name.* I wrote it again, slower, to feel it in my wrist.

We didn't read them out loud, either. Some things don't need an audience to be real.

✦ ✦ ✦

The afternoon drifted toward pair conversations. People walked the path through the grove, two by two, the way grief likes to go when it's brave. I walked with Mary. The ground was uneven, and she chose each step with care, which seemed like a metaphor she'd earned the right to live by.

"He said I was breaking the covenant by asking for space," she said. "But a covenant without mercy is a cage." She stopped beside a stone wall and laid both hands on it. "I thought God wanted me small. I was wrong."

"What do you think He wants?" I asked.

She thought longer than people usually allow themselves to think before answering. "Trust," she said finally. "Not of people who have not earned it. Of Himself. Trust that He is not the man who used His name to keep me quiet."

We stood there until that sentence took root.

Back under the teepee, Emily was telling Trinity how she jumps at soft sounds. "I hear a spoon in the sink, and my body does the math," she said. "How it might escalate. The routes out. The words to calm it."

"Of course," Trinity said. No, *why would you?* No, *have you tried?* Just *of course.* "Your nervous system is a brilliant guard dog," she added. "It learned to patrol. Now we teach it to nap when the gate is closed."

Emily laughed, first with surprise, then with gratitude. "How?"

"Practice," Trinity said. "Small, boring safety over and over." She pointed to the journal page Emily still held. "You've already started."

Sarah asked if she could try saying something out loud that felt dangerous. "What if no one deserves my immediate trust?" she said, her hands shaking. "What if they earn it, slowly, over time? What if that's love, too?" She looked like she expected a gavel to fall.

No one said anything. We gave her space. Sometimes, space is better than advice.

"Try the words on," Trinity said. "See how they fit in your mouth."

Sarah nodded. "Okay." She swallowed. "I can't rebuild trust right now." She paused, searching. "But I can rebuild my peace." The sentence wobbled and then found its legs. She repeated it, stronger. "I can't rebuild trust right now, but I can rebuild my peace."

A collective loosening moved through the room. People didn't clap. They didn't need to. You could feel a boundary settle into place, as gentle and firm as a well-built gate.

✦ ✦ ✦

As the sun's rays grew slanted, we talked about the two voices the world offers the wounded. One says, *Move on. It's weak to dwell.* The other voice says, *Weep. Bring it to God. Let Him restore.*

We knew both. Many of us had tried the first until our backs hurt. The second felt slower and less glamorous. It also felt like oxygen.

"Grieving doesn't trap you," Mary said, her eyes shining. "It helps you break free without causing harm."

"Forgiveness isn't pretending," Emily added. "It's refusing to drag the anchor forever."

"Boundaries are not revenge," Sarah said. "They're about taking care of yourself." She smiled, small and real. "I'm learning."

Before dinner, Trinity asked us to pair off and practice a few sentences aloud. The goal is not to weaponize them, but to make them familiar. "Say them to the air," she said. "Let your own ears hear your own mouth stand up for you."

We stood in little circles of two, mumbling at first, then speaking clearly.

"I need time to heal before I decide what trust will look like here."

"I will no longer argue with someone about what I feel."

"This conversation isn't respectful. I'm stepping away."

"My peace is mine to protect."

Hearing my voice carry words like that felt like watching a child cross a street alone for the first time, realizing he knows how.

Evening came fast. The lanterns' halos grew stronger. We returned to the teepee with bowls of soup and sat on rugs, elbows touching in the happy way people sit after a day of work that no one can see, but everyone can feel.

Someone set a small drum by the lanterns again and thumped it with the side of their hand, just enough to make the air say *yes, yes, yes.*

Trinity opened the Bible again. "There's a promise I want to place beside what we've given up today," she said. She didn't recite a translation. She spoke as if it were a vow someone had made to her personally, and she was relaying it to friends. "Where shame sat, God gives a double share of honor. Where disgrace tried to write the last line, He writes joy."

We let it land, not asking for timestamps and verse numbers. The promise knew its way around the room.

She set the book down and looked at us one by one. "I know some of you were told to rush. To forget. To be tough." She shook her head gently. "Today, you were brave instead. You felt the feeling that you were trying to ignore. You gave it space to be expressed. And finally, when it has fully been expressed through your body, through the words that you write, and the tears that the world told you to suppress, is when you can finally start releasing betrayal trauma. It's not weak to show the emotions that hurt you. It's strength."

We closed our eyes, not because it makes prayer work better, but because the darkness behind our eyelids matched the honest dark of the day. It felt right to let the two talk.

Trinity prayed. It wasn't the kind of prayer that builds a staircase to impress God with vocabulary, but the kind you can say on a tile floor with your back against a cabinet. "God, you see every drop. You saw the kiss that betrays, the hand that hid the phone, the smile that lied, the promise made with no bones to hold it up. You saw the child counting breaths at the table. You saw the woman obeying herself into a corner. Thank you for not shaming us for surviving. Thank you for leading us into living. Give double where shame tried to take. Bind what is broken. Teach our bodies the sound of safety. Amen."

We sat a while longer, the way you do after a good meal when no one can convince anyone else to stand.

Later, as we walked to our rooms, Emily matched my pace. "Do you think it's possible?" she asked, her voice low like she didn't want to scare the question away. "To trust again without becoming the person who trusts too fast?"

"I think trust is a garden," I said, surprised to hear the sentence come out to meet her. "Not a switch. You plant it. You water it. You see if it grows. You don't hand someone the harvest on the first day."

She nodded, relief and patience holding hands. "Okay," she said. "Okay."

Sarah caught up. "I said it to the mirror," she laughed, embarrassed and proud in the same breath. "*I can't rebuild trust right now, but I can rebuild my peace.* It didn't sound like me at first. Then it did."

"It sounded like you to me," I said.

Mary walked past, tapping me twice on the sleeve the way a mother does when she wants you to know she's nearby. "Earlier in the teepee, I couldn't believe I didn't apologize for crying," she said, a little astonished. "I always apologize for crying."

"That's one apology you never owe," I said.

✦ ✦ ✦

In my room, I opened my journal. The page from the morning waited. I had written the grief above and the truth below like a foundation. I added one line, careful as a mason placing a stone: *I am allowed to heal at the speed of honesty.*

I sat with that until the words warmed in my hand. Then I put the journal aside and lay down, palms open, as if receiving something invisible. The wind shushed the olives. The goats' bells chimed. Somewhere, a cupboard door closed. Before I turned off the lamp, I whispered the little prayer one more time, the way a child might whisper a phone number to make sure he remembers it. "God is my refuge. I am safe in Him."

It didn't erase what had been done. It drew a small border around me, where healing could begin unbothered. As I closed my eyes, I couldn't help but ponder two questions: *Where have I been betrayed, and how has it shaped the way I trust? What might God be inviting me to release and heal today?*

CHAPTER 2

EMOTIONAL ABUSE

THE WAR OF WORDS

The morning after betrayal day, mist stitched itself between the olive trees. The mountains wore a softer face, as if they'd listened all night and kept our secrets.

The path up to the teepee was damp. Our footprints made small dark ovals in the dust. Someone had set out mugs again, and a row of oranges glowed on the table like little suns. The kettle gave its familiar hiss. A goat bell answered once again. It felt like arriving at the same place with different eyes.

Trinity struck the brass bowl once, and the note lingered like a breath you didn't know you'd been holding. "We named the betrayal yesterday," she said, looking around as if to check that each of us was fully here. "Today, I'm curious about the words that followed the betrayal. The words that kept the crack open or widened it."

No one flinched. We all knew the words she meant: *emotional abuse.* The type of abuse that slides under doors, smiles while they cut, and wears perfume. She guided us through the breathing. *Four in, four hold, six out.*

On the second round, she said, "If your body has a place that wakes up when you think of someone's painful, hurtful words, rest your hand there. Let it know you're here with it." Palms landed on throats, chests, and bellies. I felt heat gather in my neck, where arguments tend to live.

"Let's begin the way we did yesterday," she said, her voice low and steady. "With what the body knows. Then we'll let the mind name it."

The Manchester woman pressed two fingers into the notch at the base of her throat. "My voice goes small," she whispered. "Like it's trying to fit through a keyhole."

The man from Berlin rubbed his jaw. "Buzzing. Like a beehive behind my teeth."

The nurse from Toronto made a fist and opened it. "Pins and needles in my palms. It feels as if I'm bracing for a fall I can't see."

Mary lifted her chin as if to make room for breath. "A tight band around my ribs," she said. "Like a corset I didn't put on." She looked at her hands and gave a rueful smile. "But I learned to lace it."

Emily glanced at Trinity, asking for permission with her eyes. Trinity nodded. "When I hear his voice in my head," Emily said, "my stomach turns into a knot. At the phrase 'I was just joking,' my whole body goes on red alert."

Sarah's turn. She looked down at the rug between her knees. "My ears get hot," she said. "Even when no one's raising their voice. It's the way the words are arranged. The sharpness wrapped in calmness."

"Thank you," Trinity said. "If it helps, choose a phrase that lives rent-free in your head. Choose the one that returns nonstop even without your permission and say it aloud to the circle. We're not agreeing with it. We're pinning it to the board so it stops flying."

We went without order, letting each other's courage set the rhythm.

"You're too sensitive."

"You're imagining things."

"Relax. You misunderstood."

"Stop being dramatic."

"I never said that."

"If you were better, this wouldn't have happened."

"It's just a joke."

"You're making me the bad guy."

"If you loved me, you would…"

Each sentence was a small stone tossed into a bowl. The bowl grew heavy.

"I have one," I said, surprised to hear my own voice volunteer. "When I'd ask a question about something that didn't line up, she'd smile and say, 'You always remember things wrong.'" I swallowed.

"After a while, I started apologizing for my memory."

As we spoke, no one tried to fix what we felt. We were just allowed to feel. To express the emotions we kept hidden due to shame, guilt, or fear of being judged. Even though nothing was being solved, the more I named what I felt and pinned it down, the less of a weight I felt on my chest.

Trinity reached for the small leather Bible by the lanterns and rested her palm on it. She didn't turn pages or assume a tone. She simply told a story, as you would tell a friend while shelling pistachios.

"There was a man named Samson," she said, "set apart even before he was born. People whispered about him growing up because his strength wasn't normal. He could tear ropes like they were threads. He could face enemies that made others scatter. Everyone knew Samson was different."

"However, he had a weakness. It was not in his arms or shoulders. His weakness was trust."

"He fell in love with a woman named Delilah. She didn't come with chains or swords, but with soft words. Over and over, she asked him, 'Tell me where your strength comes from.'"

"At first, he played with her. He gave her riddles. He told her lies. But she kept pressing, day after day after day. The question came like waves wearing down a rock."

"Finally, tired and worn, he told her, 'It's my hair. God told me never to cut it. As long as it grows, I'm set apart for Him. That's where my strength lives.'"

"Delilah waited until he slept with his head in her lap. She called for someone to bring scissors. The sound of the blades against his hair was the sound of his undoing."

"When Samson woke, the strength that once terrified armies was gone. She had already handed him to the men waiting outside. They tied him, blinded him, and led him away in chains."

The fire cracked. No one moved.

Trinity's voice softened. "It wasn't an army that broke him. It was words, asked again and again, until his secret spilled. And it was the cutting of his hair, the sign of who he was, that turned trust into betrayal."

She let the silence stretch, and then asked gently, "Have you ever had someone's words strip you of your strength, the way Delilah's words stripped Samson of his strength? If you feel called, what did it sound like in your own story?"

"As a little girl, the world told me that words aren't a big deal," Emily said. She had a bitter laugh folded into her breath. "But it was words that trained me to lower my voice and my standards."

"My husband's favorite sentence was, 'I don't recognize this version of you,'" Mary said. "He meant, 'Give me back the quiet one.'"

"My therapist taught me terms like 'boundaries' and 'self-respect,'" Sarah added. "Before boundaries, there were only feelings. I felt feelings of guilt, shame, and confusion for even having feelings in the first place. Boundaries were so difficult to make because, with all the emotional abuse, I don't think there was any self-respect left."

"Like trying to make a bed while someone keeps lifting the mattress," the nurse from Toronto said.

I thought about the feeling in my body the moment I learned of the betrayal. Her words didn't come as shouts but as quiet edits to my story. Subtle revisions that made me believe it was my fault. Line by line, she rewrote the scene until I became a background character without a voice.

Emotional abuse can be incredibly confusing. At first, it can feel like love, warm and overwhelming. Then it can shift to a cold emptiness as the person I'd given my love to suddenly becomes distant without warning. This cycle continues, switching from warm to cold, leaving me lost and eroding my identity and confidence.

Once everyone finished sharing, Trinity set three small objects in the center: a smooth river stone, a sprig of rosemary, and a little deck of index cards with blank, unlined sides.

"Three small practices," she said. "To give your mouth and mind something to hold that isn't the old script."

She touched the stone. "First, affirmations rooted in truth. Truths that you get to speak out loud."

She touched the cards. "Second, a journal for unsent letters to release toxic words."

She lifted the rosemary. "Third, a word you'll speak over yourself today that smells like who you really are."

We didn't analyze. We reached.

The first affirmation I thought of was exactly what I wish I had told myself right when the betrayal happened and the emotions that followed, which I tried to ignore. *You're not crazy. You felt what you felt.*

Then, for the journal of unsent letters, I began with *'Dear you,'* but dropped the title because it tasted wrong. Instead, I wrote what I wish I'd said on the nights I backed down to keep the peace while my girlfriend and I were dating, leading up to the betrayal.

I'm allowed to take space.

I'm allowed to protect my peace.

I'm allowed to be loved the way I deserve to be loved.

When the words arrived, the pencil felt heavier in my hand, the way tools feel heavy in a good way because they are tethered to the earth.

For the rosemary word, I wrote *whole.* I rubbed the sprig between my fingers and lifted my hand to my face. The scent was at once sharp, clean, and green, like waking up with the window open.

Around me, the others wrote.

Sarah's face softened, the way it does when it's concentrating rather than embracing.

Emily chewed her lip, then smiled, and wrote faster.

Mary's mouth went firm. When she finished, she set the pencil down like a gavel, in a move that was gentle but final.

"Would anyone like to put a phrase in the air that your body needs to hear from your own mouth?" Trinity asked.

Sarah's voice wobbled, then stretched. "The way you're speaking to me isn't respectful." She paused and looked at Trinity, and then at the rest of us. "I'm stepping away." She cleared her throat and repeated, a little louder, "I'm stepping away." The second time fit her.

Emily whispered something and shook her head. Then she tried again, louder this time. "I'm not a joke. Don't hide harm inside a smile around me." She looked like the words surprised her, like she'd found a key under a mat she'd swept for years.

Mary lifted her chin, and there was something almost royal in the gesture. "I don't owe you my compliance to prove my faith."

You could feel the tent widen without the poles moving.

We drifted into pairs and threes to practice saying our lines to one another. It felt silly at first, then thrilling. It was like learning a new instrument in a room full of people who were also learning and doing it badly and beautifully.

The man from Berlin said to the nurse from Toronto, "I won't argue with what I felt. My jaw knows."

She answered, "My body isn't a courtroom where every feeling needs cross-examination."

We laughed gently, not *at* them but *with* them, because sometimes laughter is how courage keeps breathing.

✦ ✦ ✦

After lunch, the sky turned a soft white. The wind quieted. We sat on the terrace steps and told small stories. We talked about the jokes that landed like darts, the truths that turned out to be someone else's leash, the way we swallowed our own names to keep the peace at tables where our laughter always came second.

Nobody rushed through their story to find the lesson. The lessons always showed up without name tags and took place on their own.

We found ourselves knocking on the oldest door. "Is it really that big a deal? It's just words."

"I used to think that," the Manchester woman said. "Then I realized words installed my inner furniture that would make up my identity. They told me where to sit and where not to walk in my own house. Who to be and who not to be in my own mind."

"My father's sarcasm was funny," Emily said. "Until I learned to use it on myself and called that humility."

"People in church sometimes told me not to take it so personally," Mary said. "But it *was* personal. It was designed to make me smaller."

The line between breath and ideas thinned. It wasn't doctrine; it was anatomy. Everyone could feel how a sentence can warm a body or chill its veins. How emotional abuse can look like a joke to others, as it cuts you deeply inside.

"Words are breath with sharp edges," Trinity said softly. "Some cut. Some knit. You know the difference because your body tells you."

✦ ✦ ✦

We could have stayed and talked forever, but Trinity ushered us back to practice. "Let's give your nervous system more evidence that it can choose safety," she said. "We will go three rounds. First, speak a true thing to yourself: an affirmation to remind yourself of your truth. Then continue to write the unsent letters to release the toxic feelings. Finally, breathe a short prayer."

We moved like a small school of fish, turning together without needing to explain why.

I opened my journal and wrote my affirmation as if building a step. *I can be kind and clear at the same time. Clarity is kindness to my future.*

In my unsent letter, I wrote a paragraph to the old me who used to argue in circles for hours. *You can stop. There isn't a trophy for winning arguments where the prize is your sanity.*

Finally, my short breath for peace. On the inhale, *I belong to peace.* On the exhale, *I step away.*

The teepee held us the way a good room does, wide enough for tears and laughter to sit together and not cancel each other out. When voices got tight, the wind answered. When pens paused, someone's bracelet chimed.

✦ ✦ ✦

As late afternoon gave way to evening, Trinity lit a candle and set it between the stones that rimmed the center. "We named the harm," she said. "We spoke into it. Now, I want to bring some healing to it."

She glanced down at the open Bible, then looked back at us. "There's a verse that says, 'Reckless words pierce like a sword, but the tongue of the wise brings healing.' It's from Proverbs," she said. "It's a reminder that what we say can either wound or help someone heal." She didn't quote it to sound wise or polished. She said it gently, like someone passing you something warm and real to hold.

We closed our eyes. The candle served as a small sun. The tent moved with our breath.

"I'm going to guide us through a short reflection," Trinity said softly, her voice almost blending with the sound of the crickets. "Nothing formal, just a way to listen to what your heart is already saying. If you'd like, say one word you're ready to let go of. Choose something someone once said about you that isn't true. Then, share one word you're ready to take back."

We went one by one, around and around, until the small pile of words in the center felt like a heap of old coats at a door.

"Too much," Sarah said. "Enough."

"Stupid," Emily said. "Wise."

"Submissive," Mary said, but then shook her head and replaced it. "Small. Loved."

"Crazy," I said. "Clear."

"Dramatic," said the woman from Cape Town. "Tender."

"Cold," the man from Berlin said. He looked down at his hands. "Steady."

The words felt like putting things back where they belonged. There wasn't a lesson or a big takeaway at the end. Just a quiet conversation, warm soup in our hands, and bread being shared around the table.

As we ate, we talked about ordinary things. The goat that always wandered too far. The way the terrace collected the sun during the day and gave it back at night. Which airport had the best coffee? Sometimes, healing needed the texture of a regular evening to persuade the nervous system that it can survive its own softness.

On the walk back to the rooms, Emily came up beside me, keeping her steps small to match mine. "Today felt different," she said. "Like something inside me finally started to glow again."

"What changed?" I asked.

"I heard my dad's old voice in my head," she said, looking at the path. "Instead of arguing with it, I just said my sentence over it. Not angrily, more like changing a radio station." She smiled at the dark. "My stomach didn't knot."

Sarah caught up, tucking her hair behind her ear. "I practiced in the mirror again," she said, a little sheepish but still proud. "That line about stepping away. My face didn't do that apologizing thing." She demonstrated and showed me how her chin remained steady, her eyes staying level. "I looked like someone I would trust."

Mary passed us with measured dignity. She wore that dignity like a coat she had finally chosen for herself. She touched my sleeve with two fingers. "He messaged," she said, lifting her phone and lowering it. "I wrote him an angry letter releasing all of the toxic emotions inside, but I didn't send it. I just let it be. Then I lit a candle and read my new word out loud to myself: Loved." She pressed her lips together and nodded once. "I didn't answer him. I answered me."

✦ ✦ ✦

Back in my room, the journal waited on the table. I leafed through the pages from the last two days and saw the grief I wrote that didn't try to be noble. I saw the truth sentence that didn't try to be clever. And I saw the unsent letter that untied a knot I thought only the other person could loosen.

Beneath it, I wrote today's date and a small inventory of words. On one side, I wrote words that left me weaker. *You remember wrong.* "Relax." *It's just a joke.*

On the other side, I wrote words that gave my legs strength. *I can be kind and clear. The way you're speaking isn't respectful, so I'm stepping away. I'm allowed to protect my peace.*

I put the pencil down and rubbed the rosemary sprig until it crumbled in my hands, and the aroma filled the air in my room. Outside, the wind ran its fingers through the trees. The goats muttered about nothing. The sea hushed the hillside from far away.

I lay back with my palms open and felt the day around me. I didn't think about the past or the compromises I had made with people who no longer wanted to be with me. Instead, I thought about the small moments that made me feel at home: saying a sentence out loud that felt right; choosing not to reply; writing what I had once kept to myself and expressing it fully; letting scripture be with me like a quiet friend who brings soup and doesn't comment on the mess.

I remembered Samson in the old story, his head in someone's lap, lulled by questions into handing over what made him himself. Then I remembered another scene: a room of people with soft voices and spines, singing truth to their own bones. It felt like the opposite of a lullaby. It felt like waking.

Before I turned off the lamp, I whispered a small blessing from my mouth, as I had done the day before when I blessed my heart. *Let my words be medicine where I can, a door where I must, and a quiet that heals more than talk.*

As I dozed off to sleep, I heard the voice in the back of my mind reflect. *What words still echo in me that are not my words, and what new words will I choose to carry tomorrow?*

CHAPTER 3

NARCISSISM

ESCAPING THE SNARE

T he day we turned toward the word *narcissism*, the mountains felt closer. It was as if they'd shuffled their chairs to the edge of the terrace to listen in. Low clouds dragged their sleeves along the hills.

Trinity struck the brass bowl once and let the note fade into the canvas. "We named betrayal," she said, meeting our eyes one by one. "We stood up to reckless emotional abuse. Today, we will stand before the kind of love that makes you small while telling you, 'You're special.' Narcissism."

Nobody laughed. The phrase landed. We knew it before we named it.

She took us through the breathing, *four in, four hold, six out,* until the fluttering inside my ribs settled and the back of my neck loosened. "If your body wakes up when it hears this word," she said, "put a hand where it wakes. Let that place know you're with it."

Hands went to throats, chests, and bellies. I felt the spot above my sternum. That's where the feeling was for me. There was pressure, as if someone had found a bruise and wouldn't let go.

"Let's start with what the body knows," Trinity said. "Then the stories can arrive when they're ready."

The woman from Cape Town rolled her shoulders and winced. "Right here," she said. "Like I'm trying to make myself narrow enough to fit into a sentence he wrote for me."

The man from Berlin touched his temples. "Fog," he said. "And a hum, like I'm sitting under power lines."

The nurse from Toronto laid both palms over her ribs. "Held breath," she whispered. "Like I've been underwater longer than I say out loud."

Mary traced the seam where her collar met her neck. "Weight on my chest," she said quietly. "Not with grief, but expectation. The kind that never runs out."

Emily tapped her fingers against her knee and then stilled them. "That feeling in my stomach like I suddenly missed a step."

Sarah kept her hands in her lap and stared at them. "Heat in my face," she said. "Like I'm standing in front of class being told what I did wrong, but they insist it's for my own good."

We let those body truths hang in the air the way laundry hangs between windows and makes its own small flag.

"Now, we will have stories," Trinity said. "No lessons. Just rooms we've lived in."

I went first. The words were already queued, and I knew they'd start misbehaving if I made them wait. "I dated someone," I said, "who made me feel like I'd won the lottery on the first day." I could see the early scenes clearly. There were the long, breathless messages that stretched into the night. Big plans were made after just a few small meetings. I noticed the flattering observations about me, which I had no idea she had gathered so quickly. "It felt like sunlight," I said. "But later, I realized I was a plant being forced under a lamp."

We all smiled the sad smile of recognition.

"Everything was 'we,'" I went on. "*We* are special. *We* are different. *We* don't need boundaries because *we* understand each other." I shrugged. "Then, slowly, *we* became *I*... at least, when she was speaking. Not when I was."

"Next, the temperature changed when I said *no* to something. I started offering better reasons for my *no*, as if *no* by itself had to pass a test. When I asked about the shift, she cried. They weren't big tears, but they were precise. She said she was sensitive, and I believed her. I said I was sorry, and she believed me."

"After that, I studied her emotions as if I were studying the weather forecast for the day. If she was warm, I took off my coat. If she was cold, I carried blankets. In between, I forgot my own skin." I noticed my hands curling into fists on my knees. I opened them and put my palms down, flat. Hearts nodded around the circle. It wasn't applause. It was the *same*.

Sarah tucked her hair behind her ear and took a breath like a diver. "My ex-husband turned me into a mirror," she said. "When he liked what he saw, I got love that felt like fireworks. When he didn't, I got silence that felt like winter." Her mouth bent, an old grief making a new shape. "I learned to contort. To catch the light just so." She looked at the rug. "One day, I realized the only time I recognized myself was when nobody else was home."

Emily pulled her sleeves down over her hands. "My dad could be the most charming man in any room," she said. "Strangers would tell me how lucky I was. At home, he told long stories about his sacrifices and his burdens. I learned to nod with the right amount of admiration. If I made a mistake, he told me about the way my mother disappointed him that same year, as if genetics had already made me guilty of things I didn't even do."

She exhaled and looked at the lanterns. "He'd bless me and bruise me in the very same sentence."

Mary's smile was tired and kind all at once. "Mine told me God had made him the head of the family," she said. "But then I blinked and realized that I was no longer his partner. I was his servant." Her gaze settled on a spot just beyond us. "He praised me when people were in the room, but punished me in private when there was no one else around. When I made myself smaller, he called it humility. When I asked for air, he called it rebellion."

The teepee listened. The wind ran a hand through the grove, and the leaves flashed their pale undersides.

The more we talked, the more apparent the red flags were, and exactly what to look for if we ever find ourselves in another relationship with a narcissist. The early flood of attention. The slow subtraction when you stopped orbiting perfectly. The way your own needs began to feel like audacity. The sense that you were never quite safe unless you were approving.

Trinity rested her palm on the small leather Bible. She didn't change her cadence. She didn't put on a story voice.

"There was a king named Saul," she said. "He had been chosen, anointed, lifted high above his people. At first, he led with courage. But over time, the crown grew heavier than his heart could carry. He began to love the sound of his own name more than the sound of God's voice."

She glanced around the circle, making sure each of us was with her.

"Then came David. He was a young shepherd boy. He played music that soothed Saul's tormented spirit. Later, he faced the giant Goliath when no one else would, and God gave him victory."

"People began to sing about David. 'Saul has killed his thousands, and David his tens of thousands!' It was just a song, but Saul heard it like a death sentence. Instead of seeing David as a gift to the nation, he saw him as a threat to his throne."

Her eyes lowered for a moment, as if watching it play out. "Jealousy turned into fear. Fear into rage. Saul picked up spears and hurled them at David, not because David had done him wrong, but because Saul's pride could not handle another man shining."

"Saul chased David through the wilderness, exhausted his soldiers, and tore the kingdom apart, all because he could not stand to see someone else being favored."

Trinity let the silence stretch as the firelight flickered over our faces.

"That is what happens when a person's self becomes their idol," she said softly. "Everyone else becomes a sacrifice to keep it standing. Saul's spears weren't about David's mistakes. They were about Saul's hunger to be the tallest thing in the room."

Her eyes moved slowly around the circle. "Some of you have lived near people like that. People who couldn't bear your light, so they tried to shrink you, silence you, or make you smaller so they could feel taller. If you feel called tonight, please share with us what it has been like for you to live in the shadow of a Saul. Share with us what your experience with narcissism looked like."

Mary's voice braided in. "My husband didn't throw spears," she said. "He threw verses. The sound was the same. He used religion to guilt me into obedience, but he was a hypocrite because he didn't listen to his own preaching when it came to being loyal and committed."

"My father threw pity," Emily said. "It's quieter but still bruises."

The man from Berlin rubbed the back of his neck. "Mine threw jokes," he said. "She called me a *tough guy* when I tried to tell her I was tired. She meant, *you don't deserve to need anything.*"

"Mine... used compliments," the Cape Town woman said. "He called me wise, generous, and patient when those qualities benefited him. When they didn't, I was cold or selfish." She closed her eyes. "I learned who I thought I was based on his terms."

After sharing, Trinity placed three items in the center: small notebooks wrapped in craft paper, smooth stones, and markers. "No theories," she said. "We'll do this with our hands."

She slid the notebooks around the circle. "First," she said, "a record of red flags." She saw us brace against this and gently shook her head. "Not to obsess over, but to remember. So your memory becomes a map, not an object to be manipulated."

She gave us the stones. "Second, a simple prayer you can hold. Write a word or a line on the stone and keep it in your pocket. You can touch it when the weather changes and your old instincts start trying to negotiate."

She gave each of us a marker. "Third, a line to practice aloud. We'll say them to the air until our mouths know the route."

The room shifted from sorrow to small industry. Pages opened, and pens moved. The sound of words being written without apology is a sound you start to love.

In my notebook, I titled a page *Red Flags I've Rewritten as Red Flags Again.* I wrote:

- Everything moves fast. They plan a future before they've learned my past.

- My no is treated like a challenge, not a boundary.

- They mirror my values perfectly, until I need them to live by them.

- Apologies come only when they're cornered and always followed by reasons I should feel guilty, too.

- The rules shift mid-conversation. I end up explaining why I'm hurt, not why they lied.

- They praise me in public but correct me in private.

- I leave conversations feeling confused, wondering if I overreacted.

- They call it love, but make me earn peace.

- When I'm calm, they poke for a reaction; when I react, they call me dramatic.

- Kindness feels like currency, something I must pay back.

- I walk on eggshells, then thank them for not breaking them.

The list felt like laying down breadcrumbs for a future me who might lose the path again. On the stone, I printed *"Belong"* on one side and *"God"* on the other. A lightweight anchor. For the line, I wrote *I refuse to be controlled by your reactions.*

Across the circle, others worked. Sarah's pencil moved, stopped, then moved again. Emily's brow furrowed and smoothed like surf. Mary printed slowly, carefully, the way a person does when she's writing on something she expects to keep. We tried saying the lines out loud. Not as slogans, but as sentences we hoped would start to sound like our own.

Sarah went first, voice shaky, then found a rail. "I refuse to be controlled by your guilt." She breathed, then said it again. The second time fit better. The third time, her shoulders dropped half an inch.

Emily's turn. "I won't calibrate myself to your storms." She laughed at her own poetry and then decided to keep it. "I won't calibrate myself to your storms," she repeated, more gently, like a promise to a child.

Mary lifted her chin. "When you change the rules mid-sentence, the conversation is over." She nodded once, a queen blessing her own decree.

The man from Berlin surprised us. He stood up and spoke like a person who carries old anger carefully, like explosives. "I don't need to explain why I said *no*," he said. He sat down, rubbed his face, and laughed into his hands. "That felt... new."

We shared stories like puzzle pieces, and the picture continued to form.

The Manchester woman said, half to herself, "I thought I was difficult to love. Turns out I was easy to use." She didn't cry when she said it. She looked free and ferocious.

Emily asked the air, "How do you stop wanting the intensity?" She blushed and added, "Even when you know it burns."

The nurse from Toronto answered with a metaphor. "You teach your body to like *steady*. You feed it small, good things every day until it starts to crave the quiet. You notice how you sleep after a gentle dinner versus how you pace after a fireworks show. You keep choosing the food that lets you rest." She shrugged. "It's not glamorous. It works."

We all nodded like a chorus of plants being watered.

Trinity rested her hand on the Bible. "You know that verse about fruit?" she said. "Jesus said you can tell what kind of tree it is by the fruit it bears, not by the words painted on the bark." She looked around the circle. "It's the same with people. You don't have to analyze or label them. Just pay attention to the fruit, the patterns, the outcomes, the energy that grows around them. That's not judgment. That's discernment. Knowing this, what fruit did your relationship bear?"

"Mine bore fear as the fruit," Mary said. "Not patience."

"Mine bore confusion," Sarah responded. "Not clarity."

"Mine bore admiration for a father who never once asked me a curious question," Emily said. "Not love."

"My jaw bore pain," the Berlin man added. "Not peace."

The comparisons were as quiet and sharp as a knife that cuts a rope from your wrists. It wasn't about shaming anyone. It was about stopping the lie that our feelings don't matter. We have the power to choose how we want to be treated in a relationship. That we know our own self-worth and not to be belittled by someone else, and to be guilted into thinking that the problems in the relationship are our fault.

✦ ✦ ✦

As had become our routine, Emily fell into step beside me on the path back to our rooms, eager to talk about the day. "When I wrote my list," she said, "I realized I'd ignored the same red flags in different people. Reliving the same painful mistakes in my relationship repeatedly."

"What will you do next time?" I asked.

She patted the stone in her pocket. "I'll check my fruit. I'll check theirs." She grinned into the dark.

Sarah caught up, then slowed to match us. "I used to accept apologies like payment," she said. "Tonight, I realized the only currency that matters to me now is change."

Mary walked a few steps ahead, her back straight. She turned just enough for her voice to carry. "I asked God to make me less gullible," she said. "He made me more discerning instead." She touched her chest. "It feels... different. Not hard. Just clear."

In my room, I sat down, opened my journal, and flipped to the day's page. The red flags looked like a city map of all the places I'd been mugged. I added one more at the bottom. *I feel small around them and call it safety.*

Then I wrote a small, stubborn blessing over the mess. *I'm learning to prefer slow gardens to firework fields. I'm learning to test fruit, not slogans about who people say they are. I'm learning to walk away when the price of staying is myself. I belong to God.*

The stone clicked warm in my palm. I slipped it into my pocket even though I was about to sleep. I lay back and watched the ceiling for a while, which in that room felt like watching the inside of a seashell. As I fell asleep, I reflected: *How has self-centered love shaped my story? And what truer word am I willing to believe about who I am?*

CHAPTER 4

GENERATIONAL TRAUMA

BREAKING THE CHAINS

T rinity rang the brass bowl once. The sound hung in the canvas and then softened like breath. "Today," she said, "let's sit with the families we came from and with the families we're becoming. We will also go over generational trauma and the patterns that repeat when we are not conscious of the unhealthy habits we've adopted."

No drama in her voice. Just an invitation, as if she'd opened a door and stepped aside. We settled with blankets over knees, mugs warming hands. The teepee took a slow breath with the wind.

"Let's take a breath. Four seconds in, four seconds hold, six seconds out," she said. We followed. By the third round, my shoulders had found the floor. "As we breathe," she added, "notice where your body wakes when you think of home."

Hands drifted to throats, chests, and bellies. Mine went to the place just under my chest where old stories tend to sit and mutter.

"Let's begin with the body," Trinity said, "before we add words."

The Manchester woman touched the hollow at her collarbone. "A tight collar," she whispered. "Stiff."

The nurse from Toronto pressed her palm to her stomach. "A knot," she said. "Not pain, but anticipation."

The man from Berlin rolled his shoulders as if shrugging off a coat. "A weight," he said. "Like someone draped a wet blanket and said it was love."

Mary set her hand over her heart. "A room with the lights off," she said. "I know the furniture by memory, but I still bump my knee."

Emily blew out her cheeks, flushing as she exhaled. "Loud quiet," she said. "Like everything is silent, but the silence is screaming."

Sarah stared at her hands and flexed them once. "Ready," she said. "Always ready. Like the sound of keys in the door meant 'choose a role.'"

We let the bodies' languages hang in the air like laundry on a line. It was humble, and ordinary, and told the truth without flourish.

Trinity nodded. "Thank you," she said. "If you want, choose a sentence you learned about love or safety growing up. Not a whole story. Just the rule your body still follows."

We went without order.

"Don't need too much."

"Be useful."

"Stay small. It goes better."

"If you're perfect, you're safe."

"Don't ask questions."

"Keep secrets to keep peace."

"My feelings are last."

Trinity rested her palm on the small leather Bible beside the lanterns, letting it sit there like a hand on a shoulder. "There was a young man named Joseph," she said. "He grew up in a family where jealousy filled the air like smoke. His father, Jacob, loved him more than the others and gave him a special coat, bright, impossible to miss. His brothers saw the favor and hated him for it. At first, they just muttered, but the resentment grew. Until one day, far out in the fields, they threw him into a pit. Then they sold him to traders passing by. That was how Joseph left his home. Not with a blessing, but with a betrayal."

The fire crackled, filling the silence. "In Egypt, Joseph's life was not easy. He was falsely accused, locked in prison, and forgotten by people who had promised to remember him. Yet God was still with him. Years later, through twists no one could have predicted, Joseph was raised to power that was second only to Pharaoh himself. He oversaw the land's food during a great famine."

Trinity's eyes swept the circle, her voice softer now. "And then it happened. His brothers, the same men who had sold him, stood before him, desperate for food. Power was in Joseph's hands, and he could have repaid them with chains, with hunger, with death."

"But Joseph did something different. He wept in secret and then came out and chose mercy. He told his brothers, 'You meant evil against me, but God used it for good to save many lives.' Joseph fed the very mouths that once cursed him. He broke the pattern."

The story seemed to hang above us like smoke curling toward the canvas ceiling. "Joseph came from a line marked by favoritism, betrayal, and rivalry. These were patterns that had repeated for generations, but he stopped them. He chose another script."

Trinity looked around at each of us, the firelight flickering in her eyes. "Some of you know what it is to inherit family patterns like jealousy, silence, anger, favoritism, or pain that seem to pass down like heirlooms. If you feel called tonight, what patterns have you seen in your family that you long to break?"

Mary's voice came first, steady as a hymn hummed while washing dishes. "In my house," she said, "the men were thunder, and the women were umbrellas. When the storm passed, we hung ourselves up to dry and called that faith." She smiled half-heartedly. "When I married, I kept a basket by the door for apologies I didn't owe. I filled it."

Emily traced a circle on her knee with her index finger. "My dad drank in our house," she said. "Then he stopped. Then he started. Each time he stopped, he got a parade." She glanced up and then back at her hands. "We performed gratitude instead of safety. I learned to clap while listening for the bottle cap."

Sarah tucked her hair behind her ear, then put her hands back in her lap like she'd decided to let her face be seen. "My mother was gentle and tired," she said. "My father was a man who could turn any room into a courtroom. If I cried, I was dramatic. If I stayed quiet, I was withholding."

She laughed once, the dry kind that arrives after tears have had their say. "When I met my ex-husband, he felt familiar in a way I called destiny." She shook her head. "It was muscle memory."

Something in me tightened at her words. I knew that feeling, the way the body walks you back into an old wound and calls it love. Her story brushed against the edges of mine, and for a moment, I felt the room tilt toward honesty, inviting me to step in next.

I surprised myself by telling the honest, small version instead of the well-edited one. "From the outside, we looked like a quiet house," I said. "But if you leaned in, you could hear the throwing of plates, the pointing of fingers, and the loudness of the silence that would shortly follow after. The fighting over money, responsibility, and the bills we couldn't afford to pay."

"I learned to fix it with mood. If I could make the room feel good, I was good." I stared at the lantern wick, black and frayed and waiting for fire. "I chose partners who would bring the same amount of chaos into my life. Then I called that chaos 'love.'"

The man from Berlin rubbed his jaw and then placed both hands flat on his thighs, as if steadying a table. "My father loved me by making me strong," he said. "When I told him my jaw hurt at night, he said, 'Good. You're tough.'"

The nurse from Toronto smiled with one corner of her mouth. "My grandmother survived things we only whispered about," she said. "She handed my mother a mindset that only thought of two things: work and don't talk." She lifted both palms. "I'm very good at both."

The Cape Town woman rolled her shoulders and winced again. "Control," she said. "A family heirloom passed down like a silver spoon. We polished it. We ate with it. We hated the taste."

We paused, not because we were out of stories but because the stories had drawn the room's outline for us. We could see the furniture. We could see where we kept walking into the same corners and how we had called the bruises our birthmarks.

Trinity's head was bowed, not in performance but as if she were listening with her whole body. "Thank you," she said. "If it helps, let's name the rooms inside us where our families still live. Not to blame. To see."

She reached behind her and pulled out paper, pencils, and a spool of thin red string. "A map," she said, smiling. "We'll draw the tree."

We were quiet in that industrious way the body takes when it knows a challenging task will give back more than it takes. We drew circles and squares and wrote names and little notes that only we would understand. *Anger at dinner. Disappeared. Smiled for pictures. Month of long nights. When the bottle came back. Prayer that sounded like an apology. Silence equaled safety.*

Trinity showed us how to loop the red string between names to mark repeating patterns. No lecture is needed; just let the fingers move. The body understands this simple language. There's a sense of control, an addiction, and the feeling of vanishing. It reveals a family secret that spreads everywhere, like something with a thousand tiny legs.

I drew lines between my father and performance. My mother was associated with overbearing worry and weariness. I often fix things out of guilt. My dad turned to alcohol to numb his pain, and I followed suit. My dad played the victim with his finances, just as I did. He also engaged in people pleasing, and I did the same.

Sarah's page was filled with careful script. She printed *charm as glue* beside her father's name, then drew a line from *courtroom voice* to *daughter learned to argue with air*. She connected *gentle and tired* to *her daughter, learned gentle and tired*, then crossed out the second and wrote, *gentle and strong?*

Emily's map looked like a piece of lace. *Made dinner*, looped to say *he was grateful, and then vanished into the garage*. It was a route her pencil had traveled so many times she could have drawn it with her eyes closed. She wrote *me* and drew an arrow to *the comedian at the table*, then erased it and wrote, *a girl at the table who laughs when she wants to*.

Mary's page was the steadiest. She wrote her parents' names in upright letters and drew a line from *keep the peace* to *stay married, no matter how loud the quiet is*. She wrote *me* and printed *obedience* with a question mark, then went over the question mark until it was thick and bold. She added, in small, neat script, **obedience to God equals obedience to harm.**

The man from Berlin did not draw tidily. He marked an X over *be a man* and wrote *be a person* beside it. He drew a little box around *night jaw* and drew an arrow to *son's laugh*. He underlined *laugh* and put a star, and then exhaled like he'd put down a heavy box he'd carried too far without a dolly.

We didn't hold up our maps for critique. We held them like mirrors.

"Now," Trinity said, "if you want, choose one red line you're willing to cut." She lifted the spool of string and a pair of small scissors. "No magic. Just a mark your body can remember."

We passed the scissors like a sacrament.

Sarah cut *courtroom voice* → *daughter apologizes for crying*.

Emily cut *comedian at the table* → *safety*.

Mary cut *stay married no matter what* → *holy*.

The Berlin man cut *night jaw* → *strength* like he was slicing the old tie with a new knife.

We placed the cut bits of string in a clay bowl in the center, between a sprig of rosemary someone had set down without announcement and a small stone with the word *begin* printed on it. It looked like the kind of altar that shows up when people start telling the truth: unspectacular and made of scrap and determination.

After a while, Trinity spoke. "There's a sentence we all know," she said quietly. "'That's just how my family is.'" She looked around the circle, not blaming anyone but seeing what was true. Heads nodded, and small, sad smiles followed. Then she added, "But there's another sentence, a much older one from Scripture. It says that God shows love to a thousand generations of those who choose love and stay faithful. It means the story doesn't have to stop with our family's pain. Kindness can keep going long after us." She didn't quote the verse word-for-word or list the chapter and verse. She simply allowed the idea to linger: healing can be our new inheritance.

"Okay," the nurse from Toronto said, exhaling. "Okay." She put her pencil down like a gavel that didn't need to slam. "I can work with that."

Shortly after, Trinity placed three small practices in front of us, the way you'd set out tools before building something: a sheet for *family blessings I keep*, a sheet for *family patterns I refuse*, and a blank card titled *new ritual*.

"Not to fix," she said. "To begin."

We wrote blessings first, because it helped us to remember that our maps weren't just hazard signs.

Mary wrote *hospitality,* underlined it, and added *my grandmother's way of feeding strangers, like they were angels who didn't need to prove it.*

Emily wrote *music,* and then added *the kind that makes you hum while doing dishes.*

Sarah wrote *gentleness,* and then next to it, in smaller letters, *I can be gentle and still tell the truth.*

Then came the patterns we refuse. My hand shook a little as I wrote *silence as safety, fixing as love,* and *being loved for being easy.* I drew a line through each like a road closed.

On the card for new rituals, we printed ideas that were as plain as bread and twice as nourishing.

The nurse from Toronto wrote, *Sunday phone basket,* and then grinned like someone had just handed her back an hour she'd lost.

The Berlin man wrote, *ask my son one curious question a day about something that isn't performance.* He tapped the card with his finger as if sealing it.

Emily wrote, *blessings at the door, hand on head, for anyone who leaves the house: You are loved. You can come home as you are.* She blushed and looked defensive and proud at once. "I want to start now," she said. "Even if it's just with the cat and me."

Sarah hesitated over her card, then wrote slowly, as if choosing each word with care, *dinner where everyone speaks once. No judgments. No walking on eggshells.*

She looked up, her eyes unsure. "In my house growing up, dinner was… strategic," she said softly. "With my ex-husband, it became silent. I want my kids to have something different. I want them to know that home is a place where your voice isn't dangerous." She looked back at the card and ran her thumb over the words. "It feels small," she added, almost apologizing. "But for us… It would be new."

Mary's ritual was the quietest. *Friday candle,* she wrote. *We bless the week we survived. We bless the weekend. We'll live as people, not roles.*

We shifted then into something we had learned to expect by now: speaking a line out loud so our own ears could hear our own mouths choose us. Trinity offered a sentence like a rail we could hold. *I bless my family, but I will not repeat their harm.*

It traveled around the circle, a simple song sung in different keys.

"I bless my family," Sarah said, voice trembling and then steadying, "but I will not repeat their harm."

Emily said it like a vow at an altar she had built herself in the back yard with her bare hands. "I bless my family, but I will not repeat their harm."

Mary said it like a blessing after a long service. "I bless my family, but I will not repeat their harm."

The Berlin man swallowed and seemed to surprise himself. "I bless my family," he said, "but I won't put this jaw on my boy."

The nurse from Toronto put her hand over her stomach and spoke to the knot until it listened. "I bless my family, but I will not raise my kids on secrets."

I said it last because I was busy convincing myself I didn't need to. Then I did. "I bless my family," I said, and something in me loosened. "I won't repeat their harm." The sentence fit. Not like armor, but like soft clothes that still looked good at a wedding.

We sat in the hush that comes when a room tells the truth in unison. The candle flame leaned and returned. The wind walked its slow circuit around the canvas. Down the hill, the goat bell counted time for a world that had no idea we were breaking patterns in a tent on a Spanish hillside.

✦ ✦ ✦

Afternoon slid into that golden hour that feels like mercy. We took our maps, rituals, and stones and drifted out through the olive grove. People paired off. They compared the new habits they would start with the family they have now or with the family they wanted to create. One idea was to have a family meal once a week without phones. Another idea was to practice asking for forgiveness without dragging someone else into it. A third habit involved telling a child, "I'm angry, and you're safe." This way, feelings and safety could finally coexist.

I walked with Mary, and we stopped at the small stone wall where rosemary pushed its green hands between rocks. "I kept thinking about the line 'that's just how we are,'" she said. "How it kept me married to an idea instead of a person. How it let me call harm 'holy.'" She shook her head once and smiled at nothing. "Today, I gave that sentence back."

"What did you take instead?" I asked.

She rubbed a little rosemary between her fingers and breathed it in. "That love can go forward further than harm," she said. "That my grandchildren can have a room with the lights on."

On the terrace, Emily and Sarah sat with their knees touching. They were laughing quietly in that surprised way you do when heavy things have been set down, and your lap feels bare.

"I wrote a blessing for my future kids," Emily said as I came near, and then blushed as if she'd been caught singing alone. "I don't have a boyfriend. I don't have a plan. But I have words." She unfolded a small page and read two lines, "May you always know you were wanted before you were seen. May you grow up in a love that never makes you earn peace." She then folded it back as if any more would be too intimate for the air. "I'll hide it in my bible. When the day comes, I'll pull it out like a long-kept gift."

I looked over at Sarah. She looked younger than the previous day. "I thought being different from my parents meant throwing out everything," she said. "Turns out I get to keep their kindness and lose their quiet." She paused. "That feels like honoring, not erasing."

When the light thinned, we carried bowls of soup back into the teepee and let the steam fog our faces. Bread was passed. Butter was softened. A spoon clinked like a small bell. A white cat settled on someone's lap and purred like a machine made for peace.

Trinity didn't call us to attention. She looked at the small bowl. It held cut pieces of red string, a sprig of rosemary, and a word-stone that said "begin." Then she looked up at us, her eyes shining. They looked like those of someone who loves what they get to watch.

"I don't have a speech," she said. "Just a promise I want to leave here, next to everything we let go of." She rested her hand on the Bible, as if greeting an old friend. "God said He shows love and mercy to a thousand generations; to those who choose love, even after being hurt. That means what we heal now doesn't end with us. It can ripple forward into our children, and their children, until the pattern changes."

We didn't say *amen* aloud. Our bodies did. Shoulders lowered, jaws unlocked, and the candle flame steadied.

She invited us to close our eyes and place a hand on our own chest, the same place where it rises when we swear an oath. "If you want," she said, "pray a simple prayer for the ones you come from and the ones who will come from you. It can be short. God knows our languages."

Around the circle, soft sentences rose and fell like little boats on a friendly sea.

"Bless my mother's tired hands. Bless my daughters' laughter."

"Bless my father's broken silence. Bless my son's soft mouth."

"Bless my grandparents' work. Bless my table."

"Bless the ones who hurt me. Bless the ones I will not hurt."

I whispered, "Bless my house, past and future."

After letting the moment sink in as the words we whispered lingered in the evening air, we opened our eyes. The candle had burned a shallow bowl into its own body. Wax leaned like a white petal.

We stacked cushions, folded blankets, and rinsed bowls. The closing of the room felt like worship and work at once, the kind of worship that uses hands.

On the path back, Emily fell into step beside me once again. "Is it strange that I feel both heavy and light?" she asked.

"Sounds like truth," I said.

"I keep seeing my dad's face," she said. "Then, right next to it, a kid I haven't met yet." She laughed, embarrassed. "I'm not even dating."

"You already started," I said, motioning toward her bible where I knew her blessing letter lived. "Families begin with words."

Sarah caught up with us. "I did something strange today," she said, almost whispering. "I messaged my dad." She looked at her hands, nervous. "Nothing big. I just wrote: *Dad, I'm okay. I just wanted you to know I'm thinking of you.*"

She blinked hard. "In my house growing up, you didn't reach out unless you needed to defend yourself. I don't think I've ever spoken to him without bracing for a verdict." Her voice trembled, then steadied. "He wrote back one word. *Okay.* And for the first time, it didn't shake me. I didn't fold. I didn't apologize. I didn't try to fix the silence."

She exhaled like releasing an old script. "It was just me speaking. I wasn't arguing a case, shrinking back, or disappearing."

Mary walked a few steps ahead, unhurried. She turned just enough to throw her voice back like a soft ball. "First thing I'm doing when I go home is buying a candle," she said simply. "Friday is coming."

In my room, I looked at the map of the generational trauma I had worked on today: a tangle of names and red lines cut and red lines left. The card with *new ritual* looked small beside it. I added one more. *Call my father once a week with a curious question, not a performance report. Ask my mother what made her laugh today.*

I wrote a short blessing for the house I came from and the one I'm building, simple as bread. *For the hands that worked and the mouths that went quiet: peace. For the secrets that they thought kept us safe: light. For the tables that hosted applause: rest. For the children yet to come: rooms with windows and doors that open without fear.*

I put down the pen and pressed my palm to the page as if to help the ink set.

Then I wrote one sentence on a clean line and said it aloud because my mouth needed the practice. *I bless my family, but I will not repeat their harm.*

The room felt larger, as if someone had moved a couch and revealed a window. I lay back on the bed with my palms open. The wind blew in the scent of rosemary through the window. The sea hushed the hillside from far off. The goat bell rang gently in the distance.

I thought of the story of Joseph, crying in a room where no one could see him, then walking out to feed the mouths that had abandoned him for dead. Not because they deserved it, but because he refused to let their choices define him. I thought of how turning toward the future isn't denying the past, but rather faithfully retelling it.

I turned off the lamp and let the dark be gentle. As I closed my eyes, I pondered the following questions: *What patterns end with me? What blessing begins with me?*

CHAPTER 5

UNFORGIVENESS

THE POISON WE DRINK

T rinity struck the brass bowl. The sound lingered in the air, settling us all around the circle as everyone dropped into the same feeling of presence. As the note lifted, the canvas of the teepee swayed with a light breeze from outside.

"We named betrayal," she said, her eyes moving around the circle to find each of us. "We stood up to emotional abuse. We traced family lines and the generational trauma that gets forced to repeat if we are not aware."

She paused, with a half-smile that knew the road ahead. "Today comes the part where we set down what we've been carrying for so long we forgot it was heavy. Today, we talk about forgiveness."

It wasn't a formal lecture; it was just an invitation. A door opened, and she moved aside.

We found our spots and followed her count. Four in, four hold, six out. By the third round, my shoulders hit the floor. "As you breathe," she said, "notice where your body wakes up when you hear the word forgiveness."

Palms drifted to throats, sternums, and bellies. Mine went to the quiet shelf just under my throat where old pain likes to live.

"Body first," she said. "Words after."

The Manchester woman pressed the notch of her throat. "Sand," she whispered. "Like I swallowed the beach."

The nurse from Toronto kept her hand on her heart. "Flutter," she said. "Like a trapped bird."

The man from Berlin rubbed his jaw and then rested both palms on his thighs. "Lock," he said. "Old lock. Wrong key."

Mary lifted her chin a fraction, the way you do when a necklace tangles and you want to give it room to loosen. "Tight band," she said. "Not around my throat. Around memories."

Emily exhaled through her nose, cheeks puffing. "Heat in my stomach," she said. "Like the word asks me to let go before the wound is even allowed to bleed."

Sarah stared at her hands as if the truth might write itself there. "Pins and needles," she said at last. "Like the part of me that wants to forgive fell asleep waiting for permission."

We let those descriptions hang in the air for a moment before moving forward.

"Thank you," Trinity said. "If you want, name the person or the moment without the details. Then say what forgiveness has meant in your head so far."

"I think it means pretending it didn't matter," the Manchester woman said.

"Or inviting harm back in," the nurse from Toronto added.

"Or letting them win," the Berlin man said, dry as toast.

Mary held both palms open on her knees. "In my house," she said, "forgiveness was the price of staying." She looked down. "And I paid fast."

Emily swallowed. "Growing up, it meant saying sorry first."

Sarah's mouth bent into a familiar sorrow. "In my marriage with my ex-husband, it meant giving him a clean slate while he still had the knife to stab me in the heart."

I felt the old ache step into the circle, put its weight on the rug, and sit. "For me," I said, "it meant losing the last thing I had left: my anger. That I wasn't allowed to feel anger, that it wasn't right, even when they hurt me so badly. I would just swallow it up."

No one rushed to smooth the edges off our sentences. The teepee knew how to hold jagged things.

Trinity rested her palm on the little leather bible near the lanterns, but she didn't flip pages. She told the story the way you tell it as if you were washing dishes with a friend.

"Jesus once told us about a servant who owed his king more money than he could ever repay. We're talking lifetimes of wages; so much debt that it was impossible. The king called him in. The man fell on his knees and begged, 'Please, give me more time. I'll pay it back.'"

"The king realized he couldn't change the past, not in a hundred years. Instead of punishing the man, the king made a shocking decision. He canceled the debt completely. Wiped it clean. The man walked out a free man."

She paused, letting the picture settle. A man walking out of the palace, chains gone, debt erased, the air in his lungs his again.

"But on his way out," she continued, "that same man found a fellow servant who owed him just a few silver coins, a tiny fraction of what had just been forgiven. Instead of showing mercy, he grabbed the man by the throat and said, 'Pay me what you owe me!'"

"His friend begged for patience, using the same words the man had just spoken before the king. The man refused. He had his friend thrown into prison until he could pay the debt back."

The fire popped. The silence was heavy.

"When the king heard what had happened, he was furious," Trinity said, her voice low. "He called the first servant back and said, 'I forgave you all that debt. Shouldn't you have had mercy on your fellow servant the way I had mercy on you?'"

"With that, the man's freedom was taken away. He was handed over to the jailers and locked up because he would not unlock the cell of another."

She let the words rest between us, soft but sharp.

"Jesus told us that story," she said, "to show what forgiveness really means. It does not only mean setting the other person free. It's about living free yourself. Unforgiveness is a prison where we think we're holding the other person, but the truth is, we're the ones trapped inside."

Trinity looked slowly around the circle, the lantern glow catching her eyes.

"Some of you have carried betrayals, wounds, words, or losses that feel too big to let go. Yet this story reminds us that forgiveness doesn't excuse what was done. It releases *you*."

"If you feel called tonight, would you share what forgiveness has looked like or hasn't looked like in your story? What does this parable teach you about the kind of freedom God desires for you?"

The Berlin man unclenched his jaw, then clenched it again, like testing a gate. "So, forgiveness is unlocking my door." It was not a question so much as a trial sentence spoken aloud to see if it fit.

"Maybe," Trinity said. "Not excusing. Not forgetting. Not walking back into the same room with no windows." She lifted her eyes. "Just choosing not to be the jailer. Handing the keys to Someone who judges better than we do."

We let that sit. The wind moved the canvas like a chest breathing. The goat bell counted something older than our stories.

"Okay," the nurse from Toronto said softly. "Okay."

We moved without order into the part where you say things your body's been saying in other languages all along.

Mary folded the corner of her blanket once and then a second time. "I stayed because people told me forgiveness meant returning," she said. "I thought God required me to be a doormat with a cross stitched on it. He didn't." She looked up, a quiet flare in her eyes. "He asked me to let go of vengeance and keep my home safe. I can do both."

Emily crumpled the edge of her sleeve and then let it go. "When my dad broke promises," she said, "I rehearsed speeches in the shower. I won all those arguments." She laughed once. "He didn't attend any of them." Her face softened. "I want to do something with this anger that doesn't keep me up at 3 a.m."

Sarah tucked her hair behind her ear the way she does when she's choosing to be seen. "When my ex-husband finally told me the truth, he did it like reading a weather report," she said. "I forgave him thirty times with my mouth and zero times with my body. The words were a costume." She glanced at the lanterns. "I want the real clothes."

I surprised myself with a plain confession. "When she told me she cheated," I said, "my anger was the only thing that proved to me my love had been real. I held it like proof. Putting it down felt like erasing the fact that I'd been hurt." I looked at my hands. "But the proof kept cutting me."

Trinity didn't answer with a principle. She reached into a basket and set three things in the center: a stack of plain index cards, several smooth stones, and a small metal bowl.

"Three small practices," she said, "for people who don't need a lecture."

She slid the cards around the circle. "This is an unsent letter. It's not meant to minimize feelings. Instead, it is about expressing a truth you haven't shared. The truth needs a voice, and it may as well be yours."

She passed the stones. "A prayer you can hold. One line. When your body wants to replay the scene, you can touch the word instead."

She set the bowl between the lanterns. "A release ritual. We'll write what we're giving up the right to hold against someone. Then we'll place the paper in the bowl and let the flames do what flames do."

We didn't debate whether rituals work. We picked up pens.

I wrote my unsent letter. I started with *Dear* and then stopped. I didn't write any names; I just wrote the truth.

I loved you. You hurt me. I am allowed to say both. I release the role of judge and jailer. I will not rehearse this conversation under the shower spray tomorrow morning. I will feel what I feel and give the part that wants to punish to God. I choose my peace. I choose my life.

On the stone, I printed *release* on one side and *peace* on the other.

For the line, I wrote the sentence Trinity had offered us in a dozen ways since we began. *I forgive you, but I can choose to spend less time around you. I'm allowed to feel my anger, but I no longer wish you harm. I release to God the hold that you still have on my heart.*

Around me, pencils moved, paused, and moved again. The Manchester woman cried quietly and kept writing without wiping her face. The Berlin man held the stone in his palm like a baseball and rolled it until the edge made a pale line in his skin. Mary wrote slowly, like she meant to keep the words forever. Emily wrote fast, then slower, then fast again, as if speed alone could outrun the ache.

When we lifted our heads, Trinity lit a small candle and placed it beside the bowl. "If you want," she said, "tear one corner off your letter, the part that names what you're releasing the right to punish, and place it in the bowl. Keep the rest. Don't rush. Your body will let you know when."

We came forward one by one, placing our torn pieces of paper into the bowl. When everyone was finished, Trinity lit a small candle and touched its flame to the bowl.

The fire took its time. It browned the edges, curled them, then found the middle. No one cheered. No one looked away. The smoke rose and braided itself into the tent air. It didn't smell like triumph. It smelled like paper.

"I feel ridiculous," the Berlin man muttered, then breathed out, and watched his scrap blacken. "It also feels like something happened."

"Both can be true," Trinity said.

"How does forgiveness feel to you," she asked, "when you're not arguing with it? Not the idea. The sensation."

The nurse from Toronto went first. "Lower," she said, surprised. "My shoulders. I didn't notice they'd moved."

The Manchester woman touched her throat. "Less sand," she whispered. "Water."

The Berlin man tapped his jaw. "It's just a hinge again," he said. "Not a gate with a guard."

Mary smiled with her eyes but not her mouth. "Less like debt," she said. "More like... choosing not to carry a ledger in my apron pocket."

Emily's hand went to her belly. "Softer," she said. "Not empty but not clenched."

We let that register. Forgiveness isn't a diploma. It's shoulders you didn't realize you were carrying, lowered. It's a jaw-dropping list of fewer grievances. It's a stomach untying a knot. If someone had taken our blood pressure, I think the numbers would have nodded.

"Modern me wants to say, 'Cut them off and call it a day,'" the Manchester woman said, half-grinning. "I'm good with scissors."

"Scissors are sometimes holy," Mary muttered dryly. "But I've learned they don't cut chains in the heart. They just close doors by cutting off what you used to know."

"My church kept telling me to 'forgive and move on,'" Sarah said softly. "I tried. I forgave him with my words, and then I ignored what my body was screaming. That's how I stayed in a marriage that kept breaking me."

"So maybe," Emily added, "the middle way looks like: forgive, release, and let God be the one who keeps the ledger. Also, boundaries."

"Also, boundaries," Trinity echoed, as if blessing the word.

We moved back into practice, because practice is how theory becomes weather.

"Three rounds," Trinity said. "A prayer you can say in one breath. A sentence you can say out loud to the empty air until your mouth believes it. And a simple act you'll do when your mind races in the middle of the night with negative thoughts and replayed conversations and arguments."

She offered an example of the breath prayer. "Inhale, *You forgave me*. Exhale, *Teach me to forgive*."

She didn't insist. She let other options arrive.

Mary whispered, "Inhale, *You see me*. Exhale, *I release them*."

The Berlin man tried, "Inhale, *Peace in.* Exhale, *Punish out.*" He winced and then laughed. "Clunky. It's mine."

For the sentence, we practiced like people learning a new instrument. We were both awkward and brave.

"I forgive you. Not because you didn't hurt me, but to release myself to God." Sarah's voice shook on the first clause but was steady on the last.

"I forgive you," Emily said. "And I'm stepping away." She nodded to herself. "Both can be true."

"I forgive the debt," Mary said. "And I will not reopen the account." The air hummed. It was not performative. It was beautifully firm.

"I forgive you," the Berlin man said, almost to his own jaw, "so my son does not inherit my negative thoughts."

We wrote the third part in our journals for when our minds race in the middle of the night. Mine was simple. *Put my feet on the floor. Touch the stone. Five slow breaths. Say a prayer out loud once. Drink water. Back to bed.* It felt embarrassingly mundane. It also felt like a plan my body could follow.

The nurse from Toronto, whose soft touch was always her hidden strength, murmured, "Forgiveness lowers blood pressure. Better sleep. Less inflammation. Less anxiety." She shrugged. "It's not just a spiritual thing. It's anatomy." We didn't ask for citations. The room had become a study.

Trinity glanced at the circle. "There's one thing I want to say before we close. Forgiveness isn't a shortcut back into unsafe rooms.

You're allowed to keep your distance. You're allowed to say, 'I release you to God' and to also say 'I won't be meeting you for coffee.'"

She looked down, and then up again. "This is about unclenching your fist. Not handing your heart to someone who drops things."

We nodded like people who understood how difficult it was to keep your hand open without having everything taken away again.

Now came the last ritual. Trinity set a small basin of water in the center. "If you want," she said, "dip your fingers and touch your forehead or your heart. A little washing. Not because you're dirty. Because you're done holding this in your own strength."

We arrived one by one, silently. Only water on our skin, the simplest form of blessing.

When my turn came, I touched the water, cool and honest, and tapped my chest. *I'm not the judge*, I thought, not angrily, not defeated. *Thank God I'm not the judge.*

We closed our eyes and let Trinity's voice fill the quiet stillness of the air. She sounded gentle like someone humming truth from another room. "There's a verse," she said, "that says, 'Bear with one another and forgive as the Lord forgave you.'" She paused for a moment. "That doesn't mean staying where you're being hurt. It doesn't mean pretending nothing happened. It means releasing the weight so it no longer chains you. Forgiveness isn't about excusing the harm; it's about walking out of the cell it built around you."

We remained silent, not in shock, but in peace.

On the path back to our rooms, Emily matched my pace. "Do

you think it still counts as forgiveness if I never say it to his face?" she asked, looking at the rosemary brushing the path.

"It counts where it matters," I said, surprising myself with how sure I sounded. "In your nervous system. In your soul. In your house."

She nodded. "Then I think I did it today," she whispered. "A little."

Sarah joined us with a slight smile that held both ache and relief. "I said the sentence in the mirror," she said. "My face didn't apologize afterward."

Mary walked a few steps ahead, unhurried. She turned just enough to toss her words back as if placing a stone in our palms. "I let God keep the ledger," she said. "I'm going to sleep."

✦ ✦ ✦

In my room, I began to journal my thoughts for the day. I opened to the page where I'd written the letter. I reread the lines, not to edit but to honor the person who wrote them an hour ago and did not run. I then wrote three things:

Anger proved I was hurt. Releasing vengeance proves I am free.

Forgiveness does not require returning.

I choose peace over my mind replaying arguments at 3 a.m.

Before I turned out the light, I whispered a line to the dark: "I forgive you." It didn't erase what happened. It unclenched my hand. As I closed my eyes, I reflected on the following question: *Who do I need to forgive to walk free?*

CHAPTER 6

BOUNDARIES

LOVE WITH LIMITS

I woke early with the sound of chirping out my window. I couldn't believe I was more than halfway through this spontaneous experience, but every day, I felt more and more weight off my chest as I released all of the pain I had been carrying in my heart. I walked down the path to the teepee, wondering what concepts Trinity was going to teach us today. As I ducked my head under the entrance of the teepee flaps and sat down with legs crossed in a half-lotus position, Trinity began to talk.

"We told the truth about betrayal," she said, looking around the circle to find each of us. "We stood up to emotional abuse. We traced the patterns in our families. Today, we will see what love looks like when it has a spine."

She didn't say the word *boundaries* yet. She let it arrive on its own.

We settled in. Trinity led the breathing. *Four in, four hold, six out.* Until the flutter behind my ribs perched instead of flapping.

"As you breathe," she said, "notice where your body wakes when you think about saying *no*."

Hands drifted to throats, chests, and bellies. My hand found the spot just under my collarbone where my *no* usually goes to hide.

"Body first," she said. "Words later."

The Manchester woman touched the hollow of her throat. "Small voice," she whispered. "Like I'm trying to speak through a keyhole."

The nurse from Toronto pressed her palm to her stomach. "Cold," she said. "And then heat."

The man from Berlin rubbed his jaw and then steadied his hand. "Clamp," he said. "Like a car jack under my tongue."

Mary raised her chin a fraction, making room for air. "Tight band," she said. "Like someone else laced me. Not me."

Emily exhaled, cheeks puffed. "Buzzing in my hands," she said. "Like my body wants to run while my mouth smiles."

Sarah looked at her fingers spread on her knees. "A tilt," she said. "Like the floor leans towards *yes,* and I have to lean hard to stay upright."

We let the body speak in small, honest sentences.

"Thank you," Trinity said. "If it helps, tell the circle one request you wanted to refuse but didn't. No details that endanger you; just the moment you swallowed your *no*."

"I covered a fourth double shift," the nurse from Toronto said softly. "I told them it was fine."

"My father asked me to drop everything to help him move a

sofa," Emily said. "He called me after two months of silence. I went."

"My ex-husband asked for intimacy right after a week of ice," Sarah said. "I said yes. My body said nothing."

"A church leader asked me to lead three ministries." Mary's small smile held both aching and humor. "I said I was honored. Then I forgot where I had put my own life."

I surprised myself. "My ex texted at midnight," I said. "Said she needed to process. I put on my shoes. I was in the car before I asked myself who had asked me to be a midnight therapist."

We didn't flinch from the absurdity. We acknowledged that odd instinct. Save the situation, even at the cost of your body.

Trinity rested her palm on the little leather Bible by the lanterns. She didn't open the Bible. She spoke like someone telling a story while cutting fruit.

"There was a man named Nehemiah," she said. "He heard that Jerusalem, the holy city of his ancestors, was lying in ruins. The walls were torn down, and the gates were burned. Without walls, the people lived in constant fear since any enemy could now wander in. There was no line between home and danger."

She glanced around the circle.

"Nehemiah prayed and then acted. He requested the king's permission to return to Jerusalem and rebuild. Upon arrival, he examined the broken streets at night. He saw the rubble, the gaps, and the scorched gates. Then he gathered the people and said, 'Let us rise up and build.' And they began to build, stone by stone, family by family."

Her hands made a slow motion, as if setting one stone on another.

"Not everyone was glad. Some mocked them. Others threatened to attack. So, the people worked with one hand holding a trowel to lay the stones and the other gripping a sword to defend themselves. They didn't build walls to hide from the world; they built them so that life inside could flourish again. A wall wasn't rejection. It was protection. A gate wasn't cruelty; it was clarity. *This* may come in. *This* must stay out."

She let the picture hang in the air before us. Dust rising, children carrying baskets of rubble, mothers mixing mortar, men setting stones while watching the horizon for enemies.

"Boundaries," she said softly, "are like those walls and gates. They don't mean you hate what's outside. They mean you care for what's inside. Boundaries are how love can rest without fear."

The fire snapped, and her eyes lifted to us.

"Some of you know what it's like to live without walls, in a situation where anyone can walk in, demand, take, or harm. Some of you are learning to build gates that can open with welcome and close with strength. If you feel called tonight, please share with us. What has your journey with boundaries looked like? And what does Nehemiah's story teach you about the courage it takes to build them?"

Mary went first. Her voice was steady, as with someone who has rebuilt a few walls already. "For years, I believed saying *no* meant I wasn't loving. So, I said *yes* until the *yes* stopped being love and became fear. People clapped. I called it obedience. My body called it exhaustion." She smiled, wry and kind. "When my counselor asked me what I wanted, I told him I wanted what would make everyone else happy."

The Berlin man cleared his throat. "My father taught me that a man carries more than he can," he said. "I thought that meant 'don't feel.' So, I said *yes* to everything until my son started doing my face in miniature: tight jaw, no voice. I looked at him and saw my *no* living there, trapped."

Emily picked at the cuff of her sweater and then set her hands down. "When my dad calls," she said, "I answer. I drive. I fix. He says, 'You're a lifesaver,' and I feel ten years old and glowing. Then I go home and shake." She looked at the rug between her knees. "I want to love him without abandoning myself."

Sarah started to tuck her hair behind her ear, but then didn't. "My ex-husband would message me about his feelings in the middle of the night," she said. "He'd tell me I was the only one who ever understood him. I took it like a medal. The medal turned out to be a leash."

I allowed my own small confession into the circle. "I used to think a boundary was a wall I put up because I was scared," I said. "Now I think it might be a gate I tend because I care. That sounds neat, though it feels messy."

The teepee held the mess without trying to sweep.

Trinity slid three simple things into the middle: a stack of index cards, a handful of smooth stones, and a coil of thin twine.

"Let's give our hands something to do," she said. "First: a *yes*/*no* audit. Two columns. What gets my yes? What earns my no? We're not doing *guilt*. We're doing *clarity*."

We lowered our heads and began to write.

My list looked like this:

YES

- Work that supports my health, not depletes it.

- Conversations where both people listen.

- Relationships that repair, not repeat.

- Rest that doesn't need to be earned.

- Projects with meaning and a clear finish line.

- People who speak truth with gentleness.

- Environments where calm is normal, not rare.

- Commitments that align with my values, not my fears.

- Growth that doesn't cost my peace.

- Time spent where presence matters more than performance.

NO

- Midnight therapy sessions disguised as conversations.

- "Urgent" favors that ignore my time.

- Jokes that sting and get excused as love.

- Meetings built on guilt instead of purpose.

- Carrying the emotional weight for everyone else.

- Explaining myself to people committed to misunderstanding.

- Being punished for having needs.

- Staying where peace always feels like negotiation.

- Saying yes just to keep the room calm.

- Shrinking so others feel comfortable.

All around me, pencils were scribbling.

The nurse from Toronto wrote, *Yes, one extra shift. No, three in a row.*

The Berlin man wrote, *Yes, playing soccer with my son. No, being his coach, if I start yelling.*

Mary wrote, *Yes, helping. No, rescuing.*

Emily wrote, *Yes, dinner with Dad that I plan. No, surprise errands when he goes quiet for two months.*

Trinity passed stones and markers around the circle. "Second, write a boundary word you can touch when your mouth forgets. Maybe *Gate*. Maybe *Guard*. Maybe *No*, if that feels like a friend now and not a threat."

I printed *Gate* on one side and *Peace* on the other. When I turned the stone in my palm, it felt like the hinge itself was warming.

"Third," she said, lifting the twine, "mark your line. Not forever. For today."

She stretched the twine into a small circle on the rug and placed a stone at its opening. "This is your gate," she said. "When you speak, open it. When you need to rest, close it. Try saying one sentence with the gate open, and one with it closed."

It sounded silly until we started.

Gate open, Mary said, "I can cook for the church on Friday." Gate closed, she said, "I cannot also lead worship on Sunday."

Gate open, Emily said, "I can meet you Thursday for an hour." Gate closed, "I'm not available for errands tonight."

Gate open, Sarah said, "I want to talk tomorrow afternoon." Gate closed, "I won't text after 9 p.m."

Gate open, I said, "I'm willing to hear you." Gate closed, "I won't do midnight again."

We laughed the good laugh, the one that meant our bodies were learning a new language, and it sounded strange and right.

Trinity didn't switch to teacher voice. She let the psychology arrive in the way we practiced. "Some of us learned to 'fawn,' or people-please, our way to safety. Today, we're trying assertiveness. The kind that honors the other person's dignity and your own. It's not an attack. It's not a retreat. It's just clarity."

She offered a simple frame we could carry on a scrap of paper: P.A.S.E.

Pause (one breath)

Assess (is this mine?)

State (one clear line)

Exit (if needed)

We experimented in pairs. The man from Berlin first played his father, offering "help with being a man." Then he Paused, Assessed, Stated, and Exited. "I won't talk when you mock me. I'll call tomorrow." He set the invisible phone down like a sword he'd just learned how to replace in its scabbard, gently.

The nurse from Toronto practiced with a supervisor in her head. "I can add one shift this week. I cannot add three. If that doesn't work, I'm still not able to."

Emily practiced with her father. First, she Paused and Assessed. "I can meet on Thursday between 6 and 7 o'clock." Then she Stated, "That's my window." She would Exit if he pressed.

Sarah practiced with her ex. "If you text me after 9, I'll answer tomorrow." She looked startled at how the sentence sounded in the air, like a small animal standing up on its own legs.

After everyone finished sharing, Trinity set down a wooden spoon and a small candle in the center. "Two tiny rituals," she said, amused by their homespun feel. "A spoon prayer and a strength candle."

She lifted the spoon. "The spoon prayer is for when you're about to serve from an empty pot. Touch the spoon and say, 'I don't owe what I don't have.' Then offer from what you do have."

She lit the candle. "The strength candle is for when you're about to make a call that shakes your breath. Light it and ask for strength. Blow it out when you've said your line. Your body will remember the start and the finish."

We didn't analyze. We practiced.

I started to wonder why boundaries are so difficult. I asked everyone in the group what the world taught us about boundaries, and the real truth about what boundaries are.

"I was always taught that boundaries are selfish,'" the Manchester woman offered, half-grinning.

"I thought that, too! But now, after this retreat, I think it means more like 'Guard your heart,'" Mary answered, quiet and fierce. "Because it's the well your life drinks from."

"I used to think *guarding* meant *hiding*," Sarah said. "Now, it feels like *tending*."

"I thought *kind* meant *available*," Emily said. "Now, I think it means *clear*."

"I thought *strong* meant *silent*," the Berlin man said. "Now, I think it means *steady*."

We let those little sentences ring like small bells.

Trinity nudged us back into our bodies. "Let's try a yes/no journal, quick and messy," she said. "Draw a line down the page. On the left, one *yes*, you'll give this week. On the right, one *no* you'll give to make the yes come true."

Pens moved.

My page said, *Yes, I am having dinner with a friend, and my phone is off. No, I do not want after-hours messages that seem like emergencies due to poor planning.*

Sarah wrote, *Yes, let's have Sunday dinner with the kids. But no late-night messages.*

Emily wrote, *Yes, I'll walk in the park during lunch, but no, I won't be able to help with Dad's crisis tonight.*

Mary wrote, *Yes, I will rest on Friday. No, I won't volunteer without first talking to God and checking my calendar.*

The nurse from Toronto wrote, Yes, one extra shift this month. No, three-in-a-row extra shifts as proof of loyalty.

The Berlin man wrote, Yes, I enjoy story time with my son. No, I do not engage in coaching when I'm angry.

Trinity then asked, "Who's your accountability?"

We paired off quietly. The nurse from Toronto and the woman from Manchester exchanged numbers. Emily and Sarah linked arms in that natural way friends do after sharing hardships. Mary pressed my stone into my palm, and I pressed mine into hers. Then we swapped back, both of us laughing at how sentimental we were about rocks.

"Before we close," Trinity said, "practice one more line out loud. Make it the one that feels impossible in your mouth because it's so honest."

We stood up, scattered around the teepee in pairs, and spoke to the air like people learning to play a new instrument.

"I love you, but I cannot do that," Mary said. The room felt the weight and warmth of both halves.

"I'm not available for midnight conversations," Sarah said. "We can talk tomorrow."

"I won't measure my love by how much I abandon myself," Emily said. "I can sit with you on Thursday."

"My no is not a betrayal," I said. "It's how my yes stays true."

Trinity placed her hand over her heart and closed her eyes. "There's a verse that says, 'Above all else, guard your heart, for everything you do flows from it,'" she said, her voice soft as the candle beside her. "It doesn't mean building walls or seeing the world as dangerous. Protecting the place where your life begins is essential. This means safeguarding your peace, joy, and love. When you do this, what flows out of you can remain pure and true."

She let the thought linger in the quiet, gentle but firm, like something meant to be kept close. She then invited us into a short, honest prayer. No fancy words; just a line strong enough to hang on to. "If you want," she said, "ask for strength to hold one gate open or closed today."

Around the circle, quiet words rose and fell.

"Give me the courage to close the gate at 9."

"Give me the softness to open it to the right people."

"Give me clarity to say less and mean more."

"Give me a steady hand on the latch."

"Give me wisdom to love with limits."

I whispered, "Give me a spine that's kind."

We blew out the candle together. The smoke rose like a ribbon, unspooling toward the canvas peak.

✦ ✦ ✦

On the path back to the rooms, Emily asked, "Do you think my dad will be angry?" She was not afraid. The question was just factual.

"Probably," I said. "Anger is what people feel when the old arrangement stops working."

She nodded as if she'd suspected this. "I can handle angry," she said finally.

Sarah joined us, touching the stone in her pocket like a rosary bead. "I set my phone to Do Not Disturb after 9," she said. "It felt like locking up the shop at closing time. Not forever. Just truthfully."

Mary walked a little ahead, unhurried, her silhouette a straight line in the dusk. She turned enough to let her voice carry back to us. "I'm going to tell the coordinator I can cook on Friday and I won't lead on Sunday."

✦ ✦ ✦

In my room, I sat on the edge of my bed and thought of the two words that I learned today: love and limit. My chest loosened. My jaw unclenched. I felt, not big. Not defiant. Just… aligned.

As I lay there meditating about all the other lessons from the day, a small devotion rose without effort. Guard my well, not with barbed wire, but with gates. Let love enter through clarity, not collapse. Teach my yes to mean yes because my no knows its name. Make my boundaries soft at the edges and firm at the posts. Let those who drink from my life find water, not a flood.

Before I turned off the lamp, I wrote down a line in my journal. Where is God asking me to set a boundary?

CHAPTER 7

SHAME

ESCAPING THE SILENT PRISON

❧

Trinity began the day once again by striking the brass bowl. She scanned the circle until every set of eyes had been found. Then she began to talk.

"We've named betrayal," she said softly. "We've stood up to emotional abuse. We mapped family patterns. We let go of debts that weren't ours to collect." She paused, a half-smile that knew the terrain. "Today, we will visit the quiet story beneath the stories. The one that says, 'It's not just that something bad happened. It's that *I* am bad.' Today, we will talk about shame."

"As you breathe," she said, "notice where your body wakes when you hear the word *shame*."

Hands drifted to throats, sternums, and bellies. Mine found the soft shelf under my stomach where old names like to hide.

"Body first," Trinity said. "Words later."

The Manchester woman touched the hollow at her throat. "Small," she whispered. "Like my voice shrinks to fit inside a thimble."

The nurse from Toronto pressed her palm to her chest. "A weight," she said. "Not heavy enough to crush but heavy enough to slouch me."

The man from Berlin rubbed his jaw, then stopped. "Heat," he said. "In my face. As if my skin remembers before I do."

Mary lifted her chin a fraction, making room for breath. "A cloak," she murmured. "I didn't put it on. I keep finding it on me."

Emily exhaled through her nose, cheeks puffing. "A knot in my stomach," she said. "Like I swallowed a stone with my name carved in it."

Sarah looked at her open hands. "A tilt," she said. "Like the floor leans, and I slide toward the corner without anyone pushing."

We let those body-truths hang in the air, plain as laundry on a line, honest without decoration.

"Now, one sentence," Trinity said. "Not about what happened, but about what shame told you about you."

Without order, we offered our little verdicts.

"I am too much."

"I am not enough."

"I break things."

"I am hard to love."

"I make messes."

"I am the problem."

"I don't belong."

"I should know better."

I heard my mouth before I saw it coming. "I am the reason people leave," I said. It landed like a coin in a metal bowl and rang longer than it should have.

Trinity's hand rested on the little Bible next to the lanterns, but she didn't open it. She looked around the circle and started talking like people do when they're not giving a lecture, but just telling a story that matters.

"There was a woman," she said, "who lived with so much shame that she planned her whole day around avoiding people. She went to the town well at noon, the hottest part of the day, because she knew no one else would be there. Carrying her jar under the burning sun was worth it, if it meant she didn't have to feel the stares or hear the whispers."

Trinity paused. She let us imagine this woman walking alone down a dusty road, head low and clutching that jar as if it held more than water.

"But one day," Trinity continued, "she wasn't alone. A man was sitting there. A stranger. He did something unusual. He asked her for water, not in a way that used her, but in a way that treated her like she mattered.

"It startled her. Men in her town didn't talk to her like that. They avoided her, or worse, reminded her of her past. But this man looked at her without flinching."

Trinity's voice softened. "He spoke about her life with honesty, not cruelty. He named the pain she carried, but instead of pushing her further into the shadows, he pulled her into the light. It was as though he took all the pieces of her story she had been trying to hide and placed them gently on the table, as if to say, *This doesn't disqualify you. This doesn't make you unworthy. I still see you. I still choose you.*"

Her hand raised slightly as if setting down an invisible jar. "And when he revealed who he really was, someone sent by God, someone who knew her and loved her anyway, something in her broke free. She forgot the reason she had come. She left her water jar right there at the well and ran back to town, to the same town she had been avoiding. To the same people she had been hiding from. She went to them not with shame but with joy, saying, 'Come and see the one who knows me completely, and still calls me worthy.'"

Trinity's eyes lingered on us. "The jar she carried every day was heavy, but it wasn't the real weight. The real burden was shame. That was what she put down at the well."

"It's the strangest thing," Trinity said, smiling. "Shame makes you hide. Love, real love, makes you run back into town with your head up."

No one said amen. Our bodies did.

We slid into our own stories. Not the tidy kind; the kind you tell when you're still pulling burrs from your socks.

"I learned shame early," Emily said. Her fingers worried her sleeve, then let go. "If Dad had a bad day, I was the joke that kept the table from cracking. Later, when I dated men who disappeared and only came back later, I thought their leaving meant I had failed the assignment." She looked at her lap. "Guilt says I *did* wrong. Shame says I *am* wrong. I got the two braided."

Sarah tucked her hair behind her ear and then didn't. "When my ex-husband told me about the other phone, he made a face like I was being dramatic. After I left, people told me I was brave. I didn't feel brave. I felt... defective. Like a product returned without tags." She laughed once, the dry kind that follows tears.

Mary's mouth softened into a kind of smile that had endured through weeping. "In my family, you didn't bring mess to the front room," she said. "You took it to the garage and fixed it quickly." Her gaze stayed steady. "When my marriage started to get rocky, I kept thinking, if I were holy enough, this wouldn't have happened." She shook her head gently. "That sentence was heavier than the truth. I carried it too far."

The Berlin man opened and closed his hands on his knees. "When I tried to talk, my father called me soft," he said. "I thought I had to turn to stone to be a man. Stone doesn't cry. It also doesn't laugh." He glanced at the lantern. "Shame says you're a statue. You don't move."

I surprised myself with a small, truthful thing rather than the big, impressive one. "After the betrayal," I said, "I replayed every scene, looking for proof that I had caused it. If I found none, I invented some." I looked at the rug pattern as if it might explain it to me. "It felt safer to be the villain than the victim. At least the villain has agency." I swallowed. "Shame dressed as control."

No one rushed to pat the air with verses as bandages. We let the room breathe the way a body learns to breathe again after holding too long.

Trinity placed three common items in the center: index cards, a piece of red thread, and a small mirror no larger than a palm. "Let's keep our hands busy," she said. "First, identify the shame story on one side of the card. On the other side, write the more honest name you're willing to practice. Not to perform. To remember."

She handed us the red thread. "Tie it around your wrist if you want. Not as a charm. As a reminder that the old story is not the only story. As something to brush with your fingers when the voice in your head gets loud."

She set the mirror down beside the candle. "When you're ready, practice saying the true name out loud while you look at the person who has to hear it most."

We didn't talk about whether it would work. We just began.

I wrote on one side: *I am the reason people leave.* On the other hand, *I am not what was done to me. I am who God says I am.*

I tied the thread around my wrist. It bit a little, then settled.

I lifted the mirror, met my own eyes, and tried the line. The first time it came out like a question. The second time, it was more like a sentence. The third time, my shoulders lowered a notch I hadn't known they were holding.

Around me, cards filled.

Emily wrote, *I am too much.* Then she flipped it and wrote, *I am a person, not a performance.* She tied the thread, touched it, and breathed. "Okay," she whispered, to no one and everyone.

Sarah wrote, *I am hard to love.* Flipped it. *I am loved without an audition.* She looked into the little mirror and did something I hadn't seen her do since we arrived. She let her face be soft in her own presence.

Mary wrote, *I should have been stronger* and flipped it. *Strength is not silence.* She tied the thread and smiled like a woman who had just found a key at the back of a drawer.

The Berlin man wrote, *Feelings make me weak.* Flipped it. *Feeling is not failing.* He grunted, almost laughed, and then set his jaw in a new way. It looked like a hinge, not a lock.

The nurse from Toronto wrote, *I am only valuable when useful.* Flipped it. *I am a person even when resting.* She exhaled, a tired sound that wasn't sad.

Shortly after everyone was done, Trinity offered the gentlest of frames. "Some of us confuse guilt and shame. Guilt is a signal that says, *I did something misaligned.* Shame is a verdict that says, *I am unlovable.* Guilt invites repair. Shame demands hiding. Today we are practicing repair, most of all with ourselves."

She invited us into the softest kind of confession, with no podium and no spotlight. In pairs and threes, we spoke about one small thing we were sorry for, not the giant thing, the daily thing. Our partner's only job was to listen and then say, "You are still loved." The task felt kindergarten-simple and doctoral-hard.

I told Sarah that sometimes I rehearse cleverness instead of being honest. She didn't give advice. Instead, she looked at me and said, "You are still loved." I believed her two-thirds of the time. That felt like a good start.

Emily confessed to Mary that she says *yes* to her dad because she's afraid he'll vanish, and also because she enjoys feeling like a hero. "You're still loved," Mary said. Emily nodded and let the sentence sit on her lap like a warm creature she wasn't sure how to hold.

The Berlin man told the nurse from Toronto that he snaps at his son when the boy cries over small things. "Still loved," she said. Then she added, "And you're repairing by learning." He blinked fast, then absorbed the sentence wholeheartedly. We didn't call it therapy; we called it simply being human around each other.

✦ ✦ ✦

The afternoon eased toward the hour when shadows grew longer. We were quietly focused, pens scratching, thread rubbing, breath counting.

Trinity lifted a small mirror and turned it so our reflections overlapped for a moment. "There's a message we've all heard," she said quietly. "Fix yourself first. Then you'll be worthy of love." She lowered the mirror, eyes gentle. "But the older truth, the one from Scripture, says something very different: If anyone is in Christ, they are already a new creation. God's love doesn't wait for you to be perfect. It meets you in the middle of the mess and begins the healing there."

We didn't argue about it. Our bodies had already begun to taste what this meant.

"Practice time," she said, with a smile. "Three small habits to take home. First, *identify words out loud.* Words that are short enough to say in one breath. Second, *one safe person for honesty.* Not to dump on; to be known by. Third, *tell the truth on paper.* A few lines where your shame voice gets translated into a better language."

We stood in small clusters and practiced our identity words like scales.

"I am not what was done to me," Sarah said, a little louder than she meant to. "I am who God says I am."

"I am not too much," Emily said. "I am a woman, not a performance."

"I am not a statue," the Berlin man said. "I am a man who feels."

"I am not loved for silence," Mary said. "I am loved for being real."

"I am not the reason people leave," I said. "I am a person worth staying for."

No one clapped. We didn't need applause. We needed muscle memory. We could feel it forming like letters under a child's hand, awkward and sacred at once.

✦ ✦ ✦

The sun slid lower. The teepee turned honey-colored. Trinity lit a small candle and set it near the mirror, as if to say: light for seeing, light for saying.

"The consequences," she said, almost a whisper, "of living under shame are many. Hiding. Sabotaging your own good. Choosing rooms that punish you because pain is familiar." She lifted her eyes. "But the fruits of walking out are many. Dignity returns. Voice warms. Friendships where your whole self is invited to sit down feel nice and authentic."

We didn't need her to persuade us. All week, we'd been walking out, or at least practicing and visualizing it. So that our body knew that it was safe to do so: one clumsy, holy step at a time.

✦ ✦ ✦

After dinner, we returned to the rugs. Trinity didn't need to tell us to be quiet; the room naturally grew silent. She placed her hand over her heart and said, "Before we finish, let's have one last practice. If you wish, lift your palm and say a blessing for the part of you that learned to hide. This isn't about scolding that part; it's an opportunity to thank them for keeping you safe and to invite them to rest."

We raised our palms to our own chests, as if swearing allegiance.

"Thank you for keeping me safe when I didn't know how," Mary whispered to the girl inside who had made herself small. "Rest now. I can be big and kind."

"Thank you for being funny," Emily said to her inner comedian. "You saved us. Now you can take nights off."

"Thank you for scanning the room," I told the watcher in me. "You can relax now. You are safe, and you are loved."

Sarah was quiet longer than the rest. Then, "Thank you for being beautiful even when you felt used." She breathed. "Come to the table. You don't have to perform."

Something in the air let go. It felt like a rope that's been taut for years, and then finally slides through the pulley and drops to the ground without whipping anyone.

Trinity glanced at the open Bible and then back at us. The firelight flickered across the pages as if it wanted to listen too. "There's a promise I want to leave with all this," she said softly. "It comes from the book of Romans, where Paul reminds us that there is no condemnation for those who belong to Christ. It means the verdict against you has already been lifted. You are not defined by what was done to you or by what you did trying to survive." She paused, letting the room breathe. "When God looks at you, He doesn't see the betrayal, the failure, or the shame. He sees someone He has already redeemed." Her voice lowered, almost tender. "In Christ, condemnation doesn't get the last word." She smiled, small and bright. "Shame can't be your name when you're already spoken for."

We sat in silence, accepting the moment. No one spoke up in disagreement, and the candle flame remained steady.

She invited us to close our eyes. "One breath prayer," she said. "Inhale, *I am Yours.* Exhale, *No condemnation.*" We breathed it together, twenty bodies learning a sentence we needed like water.

When we opened our eyes, the teepee had turned the color of a ripe peach. The white cat curled into a comma on someone's lap. The goat bell offered its one faithful note.

We stacked cushions, folded blankets, and rinsed bowls. The room tidied itself with our hands. On the way down the path, the rosemary brushed our shins and gave up its green scent without asking for anything in return.

Emily caught up to me, her wrist thread bright against her skin. "Do you think I'll need to say the words we learned today to myself every day?" she asked. She meant, *Will shame ever stop knocking?*

"Probably," I said. "But maybe they'll come with less noise. And maybe your body will answer before your brain writes an excuse."

She smiled. "My body answered today," she said. "When I said, 'I'm not a performance,' I felt my shoulders relax."

Sarah joined us. "I put the mirror by my toothbrush," she said, half-embarrassed, half-proud. "I practiced my lines twice and didn't apologize to the mirror for taking up space." She laughed. "Progress."

✦ ✦ ✦

In my room, the index card waited. I turned it over in my hands: the old sentence on one side and the new one on the other. I traced the new one with my finger, like someone learning Braille. *I am not what was done to me. I am who God says I am.*

I tied the thread around my wrist a little tighter and then loosened it. I set the mirror where the morning would find it. I opened my journal and wrote three small practices at the top of the next page. *Say my identity aloud, confess how you honestly feel to a safe person this week, translate shame to truth on a piece of paper.*

Then, I wrote down a little prayer that resonated with me from the day's lessons. *Teach me to speak my name the way You do. Turn down the volume on the old verdicts. Let my shoulders remember they are not shelves for other people's accusations. Make my life a table where shame loses its appetite and love finds a chair.*

As I lie down in bed and close my eyes, I ask myself the following question: *What shame story is God rewriting in me?*

CHAPTER 8

CONTROL

RELEASING THE GRIP

W e've named betrayal," Trinity said, eyes moving around the circle to find each of us. "We stood up to emotional abuse. We traced family lines. We forgave what was too heavy to drag. We found our gates." A small smile flickered. "Today, we will look at what our hands grip when we're afraid the world will slip."

She didn't say "control" yet. She let the word arrive on its own. Blankets over knees. Mugs warming hands. We followed her count: *four in, four hold, six out*, until my shoulders relaxed and released all of the tension it was holding onto since the morning.

"As you breathe," she said, "notice where your body wakes when you imagine letting go." Hands drifted to throats, sternums, and bellies. Mine went to the notch above my sternum where my "fix it" lives.

"Body first," she said. "Words after."

The Manchester woman lifted her hand to her throat. "Tight," she whispered. "Like a leash, but from the inside."

The nurse from Toronto pressed her palm to her stomach. "Knotted," she said. "Like a rope someone tied and never taught me to loosen."

The man from Berlin rubbed his jaw and then stilled it. "Clamp," he said. "As if my mouth is responsible for keeping the ceiling up."

Mary raised her chin a little, making space for air. "A brace around the ribs," she murmured. "Useful for a while. Heavy now."

Emily looked down at her hands and wiggled her fingers as if checking the feeling. "Buzzing," she said. "Micromanagement in my palms."

Sarah stared at her spread fingers. "Tilt," she said. "Like the floor leans towards *do it all,* and I slide faster than I can stand."

We let the body's sentences hang like shirts on a line, telling the truth without poetry because they didn't need it.

"Thank you," Trinity said. "Now, one line: what control has promised you and what it keeps costing."

"It promised safety. It costs sleep."

"It promised respect. It costs intimacy."

"It promised competence. It costs kindness."

"It promised certainty. It costs joy."

"It promised peace. It costs presence."

Once again, I heard my mouth before I planned it. "It promised order," I said. "It costs my sanity." No one rushed to fix the air. The teepee knew how to hold a bruise without pressing it.

Trinity rested her hand on the small leather Bible near the lanterns. She didn't open it. She told a story the way you do when your hands are busy, and your heart is open.

"There was once a king in Egypt," she said, "a pharaoh who thought he was in charge of everything. He had the biggest army, the richest land, and people who jumped at his command."

"When Moses came with a message from God, 'Let my people go,' the pharaoh laughed. Why would he give up control of the thousands of slaves who had built his empire brick by brick?"

The lantern light caught her face as she went on. "But when the Nile turned to blood, the pharaoh clung tighter. When frogs filled his kitchens and gnats swarmed the palace, he only clung tighter. When hail shattered the fields and darkness swallowed the sky, he clenched his fists even more."

"Each time Moses came, the pharaoh had the chance to let go and trust that maybe he wasn't God after all. But every 'no' came from fear disguised as control."

She paused. The teepee was so still we could hear the goats' bells on the hill outside. "In the end, the pharaoh's grip cost him everything, his crops, his nation, even his own son. All because he believed the lie: *If I lose control, I lose myself.* But the truth was the opposite. The tighter he squeezed, the more his world slipped through his fingers."

Trinity glanced around the circle. "That's the trap of control. The pharaoh thought it kept him powerful, but it left him broken. God was never asking him to hold the river or command the sky. He was asking the pharaoh to simply open his hands."

"Stories?" Trinity asked. "Start anywhere."

Mary was the first to respond. "When my marriage was full of tension and shouting, I became the house manager of everyone's emotions," she said. "If I could set the table just right, maybe he would be kind. If I could control my kids and shape them to be better than my mistakes, maybe God would reward me with peace."

"But I would always tend to snap at them and ruin our loving moments. I ran the whole house with two hands and one heart. My body kept billing me. I ignored the invoices."

The man from Berlin cleared his throat. "When my father was strict, I learned to push the pain away by organizing it. Chore charts. Training schedules. Perfect lawns. My son cried because his little plastic brick tower fell, and I wanted to fix the laws of gravity." He looked down and shook his head once. "He needed my lap, not my lecture."

Emily tugged the sleeve over her hand, then let it go. "When Dad went quiet," she said, "I micromanaged our conversations in my head. Scripts. Contingencies. If he says this, I'll do that. If he cancels, I'll pretend I don't care. I treated love like a chessboard and called that maturity." She looked at the rug. "I didn't notice my shoulders had crawled up to my ears."

Sarah tucked her hair behind her ear, then let it fall again. "After I left, I turned healing into a spreadsheet. Habit trackers, color-coded. If I did the right number of therapy sessions, church services, and journal pages, I'd be fixed. I bullied my heart under the banner of discipline. It stopped listening to me."

I surprised myself with a plain confession. "When she told me she cheated, I rewound our entire history trying to locate the moment I could have changed the ending. I tried to control my past with hindsight and my future with vigilance. I got really good at both. I lost the present."

Trinity slid three ordinary things into the center: a length of rope with a knot, a bowl of water, and a stack of index cards.

"Let's give our hands work," she said. "First: a visual. We'll call this the *knot*. It represents what isn't yours to untie alone." She placed the rope in front of Mary. "Pick one thing you've been gripping. Name it out loud. Then pass the rope."

Mary looked at the knot as if it were a living thing. "His moods," she said. She passed the rope to Emily.

"Dad's outcomes," Emily said. "I can love. I can't make him sober or stable." She passed it to the Berlin man.

"My son's every feeling," he said. "I can be steady. I can't be his spine." He passed it to Sarah.

"My healing timeline," Sarah said. "I can tend. I can't rush." She passed it to me.

"Other people's opinions," I said. "I can be honest. I can't curate their minds."

We passed the rope to the Manchester woman and the nurse from Toronto and around the circle. Each person named a knot. The rope sat between us like a snake we'd finally stopped trying to charm.

"Second," Trinity said, touching the bowl of water, "a *release*

114

water. Write what you're releasing on the card. Fold it. Drop it in. Not forgetting. Entrusting."

We wrote quietly. I printed in block letters: *HER CHOICES.* Folded. Held the card a second, like a bird I wasn't sure would fly. Dropped it. The card floated, paused, drank water, and sank. Around me, small paper boats met the same end.

"Third," she said, "a breath prayer for the hands. On the inhale, *I am held.* On the exhale, *I release.* If you want to add words, do. If not, those two can hold a day."

We practiced, twenty bodies rising and falling like the sea.

I listened to my own breath: *I am held.* The part of me that doesn't trust any hands but mine shifted on its stool. *I release.* It didn't run. Progress.

After these exercises, Trinity set a smooth grey stone in front of each of us and a pen with paint that would write on rock. "A pocket reminder," she said. "One word you can touch when the urge to manage wakes you up at three a.m. Maybe *Open.* Maybe *Trust.* Maybe *Enough.* Maybe *Sabbath.*"

I printed *release* on one side, *held* on the other. Turning the stone warmed my palm.

We drifted toward the conversation of how the modern world taught us about control, and how it compares to the biblical concept of control.

The Manchester woman went first, half-grinning at herself. "I was always taught that if I don't control it, it will collapse." She shrugged.

Mary's mouth softened. "I had that idea, too. But ever since this retreat started, I've started to believe in the power of just being still and letting God take control while I surrender to his plans." She said it without a preachy tone. It arrived like a glass of water after someone had been roaming the desert. "Before this event, I would always fill my mind with a to-do list at 2 a.m.," Sarah said. "Now, I think I'll just let go and let God handle it while I get some rest."

"I used to always like turning people into projects, especially my family members," the Berlin man said. "But now, I realize that this is just a form of control, and I should just let people be themselves. I can't control how they behave, but I can control how I respond to them."

After we shared, Trinity offered a tiny frame we could carry in our pocket: M.E.T.A.

- Mine. Is this mine to carry?

- Enough. Have I done enough for today?

- Trust. Who am I trusting with the rest?

- Act. If there's one small act left that is mine, do it. Then stop.

We practiced with real scenarios.

Mary took a deep breath. "My husband wants to talk tonight about 'starting fresh,'" she said, her voice low but clear. "Part of me still feels like I have to hold everything together so our family doesn't fall apart." She walked herself through the steps.

"Mine? The marriage is shared, but his repentance is not mine to manage. Enough? I've prayed, sought counsel, and told the truth about my pain. That's enough for today. Trust? I will trust God to deal with what I cannot change. Act? I'll listen calmly, set a boundary if needed, and then rest."

Emily: "Dad calls with a 'quick favor' after weeks of silence." She breathed. "Mine? Not tonight. Enough? I saw him on Thursday. Trust? God can meet him. Act? I can do Saturday afternoon. Not now."

Berlin man: "Son melting down over homework." He almost smiled. "Mine? Attunement. Not elimination of gravity. Enough? Sit with him for five minutes. Trust? Tears won't break him. Act? We can be sad and still keep going."

Sarah: "Lonely at 10:30 p.m. Tempted to text the ex." She exhaled. "Mine? My body. My sleep. Not his attention. Enough? Text a friend tomorrow. Trust? God is awake. Act? Put phone in the kitchen. Tea. Bed."

Me: "A text from her popped up tonight. Just a simple *'Can we talk?'*" I exhaled, feeling my chest tighten, then walked myself through M.E.T.A. "Mine? No. Her closure isn't mine to carry. Enough? I already spoke the truth. I don't owe another explanation to be at peace. Trust? God can handle the parts of this story I can't fix. Act? I'll delete the thread, pray once for both of us, and let it rest."

We laughed the good laugh, the one that means a room is learning to live at a human scale again.

"Habits," Trinity said, hands open like someone presenting simple tools. "Three of them today. Daily surrender, breath prayers, and Sabbath plans. Not theory. Rhythm."

She handed out little index cards preprinted with the words *Surrender at Sunrise*. Beneath the words were five blank lines.

"Write five things you'll release each morning this week," she said. "Then read them out loud before coffee. If your mouth won't cooperate, whisper."

Daily surrender:

I wrote:

- *Other people's opinions.*

- *Today's outcomes.*

- *My timeline.*

- *My past replay.*

- *Control masquerading as care.*

Sarah wrote *his midnights*, then crossed it out and wrote *my midnights*.

Mary wrote *his repentance* and underlined it twice. Then she added *My worth isn't proven by fixing him.*

Emily wrote *Dad's mood*, paused, and then added *My need to be a hero.*

Breath prayers:

Trinity offered a few we could borrow or bend:

- Inhale: *I am held.* Exhale: *I release.*

- Inhale: *You are God.* Exhale: *I am not.*

- Inhale: *Enough for today.* Exhale: *The rest is Yours.*

We practiced until the words rode our breath instead of our brains.

Sabbath plans:

For Sabbath, she kept it scandalously simple. "Pick a window," she said. "Four hours. Six. Twelve if you're wild. No fixing. No hustling. Be a person. Eat. Walk. Laugh. Pray. Let the world be the world without your hands on its shoulders."

We scribbled Sabbath windows like we were penciling in a secret meeting with a friend we wanted to keep.

The nurse from Toronto wrote, *Sunday 2 to 6 p.m.: no charting, no 'just checking.'*

The Berlin man wrote, *Saturday morning: pancakes, soccer, phone in drawer.*

Emily wrote, *Wednesday evening: cook for fun, not to impress.*

Sarah wrote, *Friday night: lights low, book, the sound of my own breathing.*

Trinity placed a box of matches by the bowl of water and some candles. "One more ritual for the strong-handed," she said, smiling at our collective profile. "Call it the *Open Hands Candle*. Before a hard call, before sleep, before that meeting, light it. Then open your hands, palms up, for ten breaths. Say one sentence out loud." Her eyes softened. "Something like: 'This is not mine to control. I release it to God.' Blow out the candle when you're done. Your body will remember the start and the finish."

We tried it right then. Matches rasping. Tiny flames. Twenty pairs of hands turned to the sky. Ten breaths. Twenty small sentences rising like birds.

"This is not mine to control. I release it to God." The words felt like a key turning in a lock I hadn't known was mine to open.

Shortly after the exercise, we discussed with the group what we believed about control.

"Control breeds anxiety," the Manchester woman said. "I haven't slept a full night in months."

"It fractures trust," Mary added. "People feel managed, not loved."

"It exhausts me," the nurse from Toronto murmured. "I keep moving the finish line."

"It makes me lonely," Sarah said quietly. "I'm in the room and not *in* the room."

"And when we loosen?" Trinity prompted, though not as a teacher. As a witness.

"I laugh easier," Emily said.

"My jaw unclenches," the Berlin man said.

"I pray more and explain less," Mary said.

"I find God in the kitchen," I said, surprised. "Not just in the plan."

We didn't need data, though the nurse from Toronto, true to form, offered it softly: lower blood pressure, better sleep, fewer stress chemicals running wild. We nodded. Our bodies had already reported the same.

After we shared, Trinity looked at the little leather bible, then at us.

"There's a line I love," she said, "that's less a command and more an invitation: Be still; know who's God." She invited us to close our eyes. "If you want," she said, "place your hands palms-up and pray one short sentence. Not polished. Honest. Ask for help to loosen control."

Around the circle, small prayers rose like steam.

"Teach me to let tomorrow be tomorrow."

"Hold my children better than I can."

"Keep me from fixing what isn't broken."

"Be God where I keep trying to be."

"Take my timeline. Give me today."

"Help me trust You with the parts I can't see."

We opened our eyes. The room had that glow it got when truth sat down and refused to leave.

Before we closed, Trinity asked us to practice one *boundary-for-control* sentence, the sort we could use kindly when the urge to micromanage or rescue wakes up.

We stood in pairs around the teepee, speaking to the air like people learning an instrument:

"I care about you. This part isn't mine to control."

"I can help with what's mine. I'm releasing the rest."

"I'm available Thursday for an hour. I won't problem-solve tonight."

"I'm trusting you to handle your piece. I'm handling mine."

"This is not mine to control. I release it to God."

We gathered again. Trinity glanced around, eyes soft and clear. "Thank you," she said. "For telling the truth. For loosening your hands. For letting love be bigger than your plan."

Evening slid in blue. We stacked cushions, rinsed bowls, and folded blankets. Work as benediction.

✦ ✦ ✦

On the path back, the rosemary brushed our shins and gave up its scent without being asked. The white cat threaded our steps like punctuation. The sky dimmed to ink with pinholes for stars.

Emily matched my pace. "If I let go," she said, and she was not fearful, just curious, "what if everything falls apart?"

"Some things might," I said. "The ones that only stayed together because you were holding both ends. Maybe they weren't meant to be a one-person job."

She nodded like a person who'd suspected as much. "I lit the candle before I called Dad," she said. "I said the sentence. He was disappointed. I didn't break."

✦ ✦ ✦

In my room, I said the sentence I'd been practicing all afternoon: "This is not mine to control. I release it to God."

And as I turned off the light and closed my eyes, I meditated on the question: *where am I still clinging to control instead of trusting God?*

CHAPTER 9

REDEMPTION

FROM WOUNDED TO CYCLE BREAKER

O n the last day of the retreat, I had to confront something that was the hardest for me to do. Ever since the betrayal, I have made that trauma become my story. I made that trauma become my identity. And because of this, I would always play the victim. I wanted to blame her. I wanted to blame the person she cheated on me with. I wanted to blame my circumstances. I even wanted to blame God. And I made this the narrative of my life and the reason why I was not allowed to be happy. Which is why when Trinity said the last day was reserved for redemption, I flinched a little bit in fear. I didn't want to let go of my narrative. I didn't want to let go of being the victim. It was so much easier to just be the victim than to do something with my life and to go out there and find someone else again. Ending up alone extremely scared me, which was why the last day really hit me hard in what I needed to do with my heart from this moment forward. Now here I was, in the teepee, shedding layer after layer of pain and fear as Trinity began the day's practice.

"We named betrayal," she said, her eyes finding each of us. "We stood up to emotional abuse. We traced the family lines and cut what needed cutting. We forgave. We found our gates. We opened our hands." She smiled, the kind that knows both ache and hope. "Today, we will see what God does with the pieces."

No lecture in her voice. Just an open door.

We settled, blankets over knees, mugs warming hands, and followed her count. *Four in, four hold, six out.*

"As you breathe," she said, "notice where your body wakes when you think about your life being rewritten."

Hands drifted, throats, sternums, bellies. Mine went to the quiet shelf under my heart where I kept the old hurtful names I would call myself, and replaced it with my new resolve to break my cycles and unhealthy patterns.

The Manchester woman touched the hollow at her throat. "Warm," she whispered. "Like a hand that fits."

The nurse from Toronto pressed her palm to her chest. "Unlatching," she said. "A door I didn't know was locked."

The man from Berlin rubbed his jaw and then stilled it. "Room," he said, surprised. "In here." He tapped his chest once, lightly.

Mary lifted her chin a fraction. "Light," she murmured. "Not absence. Presence."

Emily looked at her hands and flexed them. "Tingling," she said. "Not adrenaline. Electricity finding its way back."

Sarah stared at her open palms. "Lift," she said. "Like something is being carried *with* me instead of *by* me."

A stillness filled the air. But it wasn't a sad stillness. It was a transformative one. The kind of silence that comes after you realize just how much you have grown in such a short amount of time.

"Before we tell stories," Trinity said, "one sentence each: Not what hurt you, but what has changed in you."

Without order, we said:

"I don't apologize for crying."

"I sleep through the night."

"My son's tears don't scare me."

"I don't answer at midnight."

"I ask God before I answer anyone."

"I feel young and old at once, in a good way."

"I tell the truth faster," I said. "Even to myself."

Trinity rested her palm on the little leather bible by the lanterns. She didn't open it. She told a story the way people tell family stories while the soup simmers.

"There was once a woman named Naomi," she began, "who lost everything. First, her home. Then famine drove her family to a foreign land. Then her husband died. Then both of her sons. All she had left were two young widowed daughter-in-laws."

"She was so empty she renamed herself *Mara*, which means 'bitter.' She said, 'God has dealt harshly with me.'"

The circle leaned in. We could almost see Naomi walking on that dusty road back to Bethlehem, shoulders hunched, the weight of loss dragging behind her like a shadow.

"One of her daughter-in-laws turned back," Trinity went on. "But the other, Ruth, clung to her. Ruth said, 'Where you go, I'll go. Your people will be my people. Your God, my God.' So Naomi returned home with nothing but this young foreign woman at her side. People barely recognized her; she was so changed by sorrow. She thought her story was over."

Trinity's eyes lifted, scanning us slowly. "But God was already writing redemption. Ruth went out to gather leftover grain in the fields, just to keep them alive. By chance, or by providence, she found herself in the field of Boaz, a man of integrity and kindness. He noticed her, protected her, and gave her more than she asked for."

"Their lives intertwined. Ruth remarried, and their son became the joy of Naomi's old age. The same woman who called herself bitter was now holding a baby in her arms, her face lined with both tears and laughter. The women of the village said to her, 'Your daughter-in-law loves you more than seven sons. This child is your redeemer.'"

Trinity's voice softened, but it carried to every ear in the teepee. "That boy grew up to be the grandfather of King David. From Naomi's ashes came a lineage that led to Jesus himself. What Naomi thought was the end was really the seed of a new beginning."

She looked around the circle, letting it land. "Redemption doesn't erase the loss. It doesn't pretend the graves aren't there. But it does something Naomi couldn't imagine: It plants new life right in the soil of sorrow. It turns bitterness into blessing."

"It wasn't denial," Trinity said. "She didn't pretend the pit wasn't a pit. She simply refused to make the pit her identity any longer."

You could feel the circle lean into that line, a line that isn't a line so much as a map. *Victim, survivor, overcomer.* And then something else: Someone who, by grace, becomes a well for others in a place that used to be dry.

"What stories will you create after you leave this retreat?" she asked. "Say them as if they have already happened. Say them as if you're already looking back at your redemption arc. Say them with the gratitude you would feel in your heart if you actually became the person you want to be – the person who, before this retreat, you thought was impossible."

The room hesitated for a bit, but then it came alive.

Mary went first, steady as bread. "I used to think my offering to the world was how much pain I could carry without making a sound. I kept a basket by the door for apologies I didn't owe. Now, the basket holds candles."

She smiled, small and real. "On Fridays, I light one of the candles and bless the week we lived through. I started inviting two young women from church who are standing at doors I once used. We eat soup. We don't fix. We name. Last week, one of them said, 'I slept.' I wanted to frame that sentence."

Emily tugged her sleeve, then set her hands flat. "I don't run to my father's urgency anymore," she said. "I meet him on Thursdays from 6 to 7. Sometimes, he shows. Sometimes, he doesn't. Either way, on Friday afternoons, I walk with a twelve-year-old girl from our neighborhood whose home is loud with arguments from her parents in the ways mine was. We look at birds and name five good things. She laughs like a person that forgot she knew how."

She blinked fast. "I thought surviving was the best I could do. Now I think I'm practicing being someone safe."

Sarah started to tuck her hair behind her ear, then let her hand fall, like she'd decided to stay seen. "I host Sunday dinners now," she said. "Just my kids and me. Phones away, TV off. We go around the table, and each of us has to say one true thing about our week." She smiled, her eyes bright with it. "Last Sunday, my oldest looked at me and said, 'Mom, I like it when you talk more.' He said it like a secret. I realized this is the first table I've ever sat at where my voice isn't on trial." She exhaled. "That feels like breaking the cycle."

She breathed out. "For a long time, revenge looked like becoming so independent that no one could touch me. It was lonely. Now, revenge looks like a table that keeps a chair available for whoever needs it. Including me."

The Berlin man rubbed the back of his neck and then smiled at his hands like he'd caught them doing something right. "My son cried over a toppled toy tower that he built. I sat down next to him on the floor and said, 'We can be sad and still keep going.' He crawled into my lap. The tower waited. We built later. My jaw didn't lock once." He swallowed. "I didn't think gentleness was an inheritance I could pass down. Turns out it is."

The nurse from Toronto, facts always being her soft superpower, offered her data like a gift. "My blood pressure's down," she said, almost sheepishly. "I stopped volunteering for hero shifts. I mentor new nurses instead. I teach them how to say *no* without apology and how to chart compassionately without setting themselves on fire. Some nights, I go home and sit in the quiet and don't feel guilty about it."

I surprised myself. "I no longer write midnight monologues in the shower," I said. "Whenever the old film starts, I touch the stone in my pocket and say one sentence out loud: *I let go of control.*"

"On Thursdays, I meet with a couple of men who are two steps behind me on the same road. We don't trade war stories like trophies. We bless each other's bruises. Sometimes, we just eat food and say nothing. That helps."

Trinity listened with her whole face. When we were finished with that exercise, Trinity slid three small things into the center: a stack of index cards, a handful of smooth stones, and a fountain pen with blue-black ink.

"Let's give your hands work," she said. "Today, we make *testimony markers.*

"On one side of the card: *Then.* On the other: *Now.* One sentence each. Not an essay. A witness."

Trinity touched the stones. "On the rock, print one word you never want to forget. A word that God gave you here."

She lifted the pen. "Lastly, write a short letter to someone who is three steps behind you. The letter you wish someone had handed you when you were still in the pit."

We bent our heads. The cards were filled.

On my card, I wrote: *Then, I argued with ghosts at 3 a.m. Now, I sleep and speak truth while the kettle boils.* On my stone, I printed *well* on one side, *joy* on the other. The pen felt weighty in a good way. My letter was simple:

Dear friend I haven't met,

You are not crazy, and you are not alone. Your body has kept you alive; now it will help you live.

Make a small table. Put bread on it. Invite one safe person. Say one true sentence. Repeat next week. Your story is not over.

God is better at rebuilding than you are at fixing.

When you can't pray, breathe: 'I am Yours. You are with me.'

When you can pray, say this: 'This pain will not end with me. It will bless others.'

I will be one of those others: A man who thought midnight would last forever, and was wrong.

Around me, pens moved, paused, and moved again. You could hear the room turn into a workshop where souls were sanded and oiled, not replaced.

Trinity set a small bowl in the center and a little bundle of rosemary beside it. "When you're ready," she said, "place your *Then/Now* card in the bowl. Not to give it away. To put it where we can see what God is up to."

We came forward one by one. The cards fanned out like tiles:

Then: afraid, apologizing, obedient to harm, jaw locked, running toward urgency.

Now: gentle and clear, sleeping, saying no with love, playing on the floor, lighting a Friday candle.

Trinity reached for the rosemary and rubbed it between her fingers until the scent rose. "There's a modern sentence that comes to mind that seems different from biblical wisdom," she said, amused and a little sad. "We've all heard it: *Just survive.*"

She let the words sit. "But the older sentence says: *God turns wounds into wells.*" She smiled at us. "We're living proof."

No one drew a comparison chart. The air had one written in it. We could feel the consequences of staying defined by pain. The way it builds small rooms with low ceilings. The way it keeps a person circling the same three blocks and calling that a city. We could feel the benefits of walking out, of purpose that didn't need applause, of a legacy that smelled like soup and not smoke.

"Let's practice blessing forward," Trinity said. She took a new stack of index cards labeled Generational Blessing and slid them around the circle. "Write one sentence you want your grandchildren to overhear, even if you never meet them."

Mary's pen moved slowly, deliberately. She wrote: *In this house, we tell the truth kindly and rest without apologizing.*

Emily wrote: *Your laughter is safe here. So are your tears.*

Sarah wrote: *We do repairs, not just apologies.*

The Berlin man wrote: *Soft and strong live in the same body.*

The nurse from Toronto wrote: *Rest is not a reward. It's part of the work.*

I wrote: Our table has room for the one who thinks they don't belong, starting with you.

We didn't read them aloud. Some blessings are better overheard.

When we were done, Trinity said simply, "Habits." Her palms were open like someone presenting simple tools. "Three to take home:

"Testimony journaling. Once a week, two lines: 'Where I saw God rewrite.'"

"Mentoring. Find one person to walk with, not fix. Offer soup before advice."

"Blessing prayer. Speak a sentence over your house every Friday night, even if it's just you and a candle."

We practiced all three there, right then, so our bodies would have a memory.

Testimony journaling: We opened our notebooks and wrote two lines, dated and plain. Mine: I told the truth without turning it into a performance. I slept and didn't rehearse an apology in the morning.

Mentoring: We paired up with someone who felt like the next right step. The nurse from Toronto and the Manchester woman swapped numbers with the matter-of-fact tenderness of people arranging rides to a doctor. Emily and Sarah squeezed each other's hands and laughed, like they'd just gotten away with something holy. The Berlin man pointed at me and made a face like, every other Thursday? I nodded.

Blessing prayer: We lit a small tea light and, one by one, spoke a sentence over the air we'd been breathing all week. Nothing fancy.

"Peace to those who step over this threshold."

"Laughter we don't second-guess."

"Bread that multiplies when needed."

"Sleep without fear."

"Work with joy."

"Forgiveness that doesn't forget safety."

We blew the candle out together. Smoke ribboned upward like a psalm. I looked out of the teepee door and noticed the sky changing. The afternoon leaned toward gold. The teepee glowed. We drifted out among the olives for a stretch. People walked in pairs, the way grief and hope like to travel together, with elbows touching.

I walked with Sarah. "When Trinity told the Ruth story," she said, "I felt something shift in my heart." She traced a circle in the air. "I used to think that if something bad happened to me, it was my punishment. Now, I realize that it's God pruning me and preparing me for something better."

After our quick stretch, we gathered back in the teepee on the rugs, knees touching. Trinity set a small bowl of clear water in the center with a few springy twigs of rosemary floating in it. She looked at us with that mix of tenderness and quiet fierceness we'd grown to trust.

"The arc we've been walking," she said, "isn't neat. But it's real." She lifted a finger and traced it in the air like she was drawing a river: "Wounded. Surviving. Overcoming. Redeeming." She let the last word linger. "That last one is grace." She didn't mean it as church-speak. She meant it as oxygen.

"Before we close," she added, "I want each of us to try a line that turns our pain into a blessing. Not a slogan. A vow."

We shifted, nervous and ready.

Emily spoke first, voice shaking and then steady: "This pain will not end with me. It will bless others."

Sarah followed: "My house will be a place where honesty doesn't cost belonging."

Mary: "I bless my family. I refuse to pass them the harm I received."

The Berlin man: "My son will inherit gentleness."

The nurse from Toronto: "The nurses I mentor will inherit rest."

I swallowed and tried mine on. "I will not waste what hurt me. I will dig here until I strike water."

The room breathed *yes*.

Trinity glanced at the little bible and then back at us. "There's a sentence I want to leave beside our vows," she said, kitchen-English plain. "People may plan harm, but God can turn it toward good… enough good to keep others alive."

She set her hand on her chest. "This is not a call to glorify pain. It's a summons to watch what God can build where the world gave us ruins."

We closed our eyes. She invited a short prayer, one breath long. "Inhale: You are with me. Exhale: Turn it to good." Twenty chests rose and fell, like the sea does when it's not in a hurry.

When we opened our eyes, the teepee was the color of honey. We cleaned up together. And when we were done, someone blew out the lantern, and the smoke wrote one last curl into the air.

On the path down to our lodging, the rosemary brushed our shins as we reflected on the day we just had. The sky turned bluish-blackish with holes poked in it for the tiny little stars that started to twinkle.

Emily matched my pace. "Do you think redemption is a thing you feel?" she asked. "Or a thing you do?"

"Maybe both," I said. "Maybe it's a table you set and a sleep you finally get."

✦ ✦ ✦

In my room, the card with *Then/Now* waited beside the stone that said Well/Joy. I picked them up and felt the weight of both: the past and the gift. I opened my journal and wrote two lines at the top:

Today I saw God rewrite: A table felt safe, and a jaw stayed soft.

I added a little blessing for the house I came from and the house I'm becoming:

May the pain stop with me, and the blessing keep going. May my children, whether born or gathered, inherit rest and laughter. May our table be as wide as mercy and as strong as truth.

Then I wrote the sentence we practiced, the one my mouth is learning to trust without flinching: *This pain will not end with me. It will bless others.*

A small prayer rose without effort:

Author of stories, take the pages I tried to burn. Bind them into something that feeds a life. Turn the pit into a well, the wilderness into a garden. Teach my bones the shape of joy that doesn't deny sorrow, but outlives it. Let the next generation find shade under trees I planted with shaking hands.

Before I turned out the light, I scribbled one final question at the bottom of the page for tomorrow's honest work: *What blessing will I pass down instead of pain?*

I gently went to bed to prepare for my morning flight back to Bali. What a beautiful event this was, and one that I didn't expect to attend. And how fulfilling are the lessons I will now take with me to the new life that I promise myself to live.

BEFORE YOU GO... A SMALL GIFT

Thank you for spending this time with me in these pages. Writing this book was my way of offering you what I needed most when betrayal first broke my world: a way to heal with God, not just cope without Him.

But I also know healing doesn't happen in one sitting: it unfolds slowly, through honesty, faith, and the quiet work of showing up again. To walk beside you as you keep rebuilding, I've created a free set of printable companions to help you heal one small step at a time.

They're yours, completely free, just for readers of *Healing Betrayal Trauma.*

Here's what you'll find inside:

- **Rebuilding Trust Checklist** — practical and spiritual steps to begin trusting again

- **Betrayal Detox Journal** — guided journal prompts to release anger, shame, and self-blame

- **The 5 Stages of Heart Restoration Journal** — scripture-based reflections to guide you from shock to surrender

- **7 Healing Prayers for the Betrayed Heart** — short, honest prayers for the days you can't find words

Each resource was designed to sit beside your Bible, your coffee mug, or your quiet moments with God. Use them slowly. Print them. Fold them. Let them remind you that healing is not about going back, it's about walking forward, hand in hand with the One who never left.

You can download them here:

mikevestil.com/healingbetrayal-gift (or scan the QR code below)

SCAN ME

CAN I ASK YOU SOMETHING SMALL?

If this book met you in a moment when betrayal felt too heavy to name, and even one page helped you breathe a little easier, would you take 60 seconds to share that with someone else who's still in the dark?

Your review isn't just words on Amazon. It's a small light for the next person awake at 2 a.m., searching for hope after heartbreak. It tells them, *"You're not alone. Healing is possible."*

It doesn't have to be long, just one honest line about what spoke to you or how God met you through these pages.

You can simply scan the QR code below, or go to this link: **mikevestil.com/healingbetrayal-review**

SCAN ME

I read every single one, and your words mean more than you realize. Thank you for being part of this journey with me.

AFTERWORD: THE JOURNEY CONTINUES

If you've made it here, you've done more than finish a book. You've survived a heartbreak that once tried to rewrite your worth. You've looked at the wound instead of covering it. You've faced the silence, the questions, and the ache that betrayal leaves behind.

And maybe for the first time in a long time, you've let yourself breathe again.

This wasn't just another read for you. It wasn't about learning how to move on. It was about remembering that you were never abandoned by God, even in the breaking. These pages became a safe place to lay down what shattered you and begin to rebuild with grace. They reminded you that the pieces of your story are not wasted. Even what was meant to harm you can become holy ground for your healing.

Because I know what it's like to sit in the aftermath, replaying every detail, wondering if you could have stopped the fall. I know the feeling of loving someone who broke your trust and doubting if your heart will ever feel safe again. I know the emptiness of praying through tears that don't seem to change anything.

And yet, here you are. Still standing. Still reaching toward hope. Still daring to believe that peace might be possible again.

If there's one truth I pray stays with you, it's this: You do not have to rebuild alone. You do not have to earn love again. You do not have to keep holding what God has already asked you to release.

Healing doesn't erase what happened. It rewrites what comes next.

The last page isn't the end. It's a doorway. A daily practice of trust, surrender, and choosing to believe that God's love is stronger than the betrayal that broke you.

And if this book has met you where it mattered, if it gave you even a breath of relief or a flicker of faith, I ask you to pass it on. Because somewhere, someone is still staring at the ceiling, wondering if they will ever feel whole again. Your act of sharing could be the light they need to find their way back to hope.

Remember this: God is not finished with you. The betrayal was not the end of your story. It was the beginning of His healing. The cracks in your heart are not proof of failure; they are the places where His mercy shines through.

When you forget, return to these pages. Let them remind you of the truth: You are still chosen. You are still loved. You are still being made new.

With love and hope for your restoration,

Mike Vestil

ABOUT THE AUTHOR

MIKE VESTIL

I'm not a pastor, therapist, or expert on pain. I'm simply someone who has watched trust collapse and wondered if my heart would ever feel safe again. Betrayal has a way of stripping everything down to the bone. It makes you question your worth, your instincts, and even your faith.

For years, I tried to hold everything together, the image, the relationships, the peace that was more performance than truth. I thought forgiveness meant staying silent, that endurance was love, and that if I just tried harder, I could fix what was broken. But carrying what was never mine to fix only broke me further.

My healing didn't begin with revenge or reconciliation. It started with surrender, with realizing that God was not asking me to pretend everything was fine, but to trust Him enough to tell the truth. Healing meant letting go of the story I thought I needed and learning to rest in the one He was writing.

Today, I live simply in Asia, building a quiet life around faith, family, and peace. My definition of success has changed. It's not about proving anything anymore. It's about presence, honesty, and protecting the light God has placed inside me.

This book is for anyone who has loved deeply and been let down. For the ones who trusted and were betrayed, who smiled through pain, who stayed when they should have rested. It's for those learning to believe again, not just in others, but in themselves, and in a God who never stopped being faithful.

I don't write this as a teacher. I write it as a witness. These pages are part confession and part compass, my way of saying that your heart is not too damaged to heal, your faith is not too fragile to stand, and your story is not over yet.

Stay connected:

mikevestil.com: writings, reflections, and occasional updates Instagram: @mikevestil